$\mathcal{P}$interest
POWER

Pinterest

POWER

Market Your Business, Sell Your Product,
and Build Your Brand on the
World's Hottest Social Network

JASON MILES *and* **KAREN LACEY**

NEW YORK CHICAGO SAN FRANCISCO
LISBON LONDON MADRID MEXICO CITY MILAN
NEW DELHI SAN JUAN SEOUL SINGAPORE
SYDNEY TORONTO

For Ulysses Cortes Self—a great man.
—Jason Miles

For my father.
—Karen Lacey

Contents

Part 1
THE POWER OF PINTEREST

Part 2
PINTEREST FOR MARKETERS

Part 3
LEVERAGING THE POWER OF PINTEREST

Foreword

I've always loved expressing myself through how I dress, and growing up in the first generation with access to the Internet, I was able to take my style cues from inspirations spanning decades and from all over the world. But as a teenager in the suburbs of Ft. Lauderdale, Florida, the reality of finding clothes that matched with those inspirations was quite different. I was limited to shopping at any one of four or five malls in my area, but they all seemed to have the same collection of stores and styles. I wasn't seeing that eclectic mix that reflected my own personal style. Luckily, I discovered an alternative. Living in a town that attracted its fair share of retirees, I chose instead to explore the thrift stores, yard sales, and Goodwill/Salvation Army establishments, which were always seeing an influx of unique vintage inventory.

The summer before I started college at Carnegie Mellon University in Pennsylvania, I moved to Pittsburgh and continued my habit of thrift shopping. Soon, my dorm room began to fill with these spectacular pieces that just weren't my size or style, so with the help of my boyfriend-at-the-time (now husband and cofounder/CEO Eric Koger), I started my own website, and ModCloth.com was born! I'm so happy to be at a place now as cofounder and chief creative officer of ModCloth, where I can bring that eclectic mix to women all over the country who are looking for something to wear that's as unique as they are.

Pinterest was also inspired by a love of collections, as you'll read about through Pinterest founder Ben Silberman's inspiring story of how he built his business with passion, patience, and a great team as a base. Pinterest is quickly becoming a powerful social platform that allows dedicated collectors to organize and share aspirational content they find on the web. Who gets to have a say in what's popular or beautiful is becoming more democratic every day, and not just in fashion. Pinterest is building a growing community of (mostly) women who are enthusiastically defining and sharing the way they see the world. Like no other social network, Pinterest allows people to tell a story and express who they are with curated collections of images and items they love, to follow like-minded tastemakers, and even to become tastemakers themselves!

It was Pinterest's unique combination of aspiration and community that made it such a great fit for ModCloth. From the beginning I wanted to build stories around the special pieces I was selling on my site—first around their history, and then as I moved into selling items from independent designers, around those designers' unique stories. I also wanted to develop a brand that told a story about myself and our customer and that acknowledged a spectrum of other interests beyond fashion, such as the latest bands, books, DIY projects, and recipes. Pinterest has been a vital tool in helping us reach that girl and tell the story of who we are as a brand better than we ever could before.

And as this book will detail, Pinterest can be a powerful tool for businesses, especially online businesses. I believe that customers want to be inspired when they shop. A visual discovery platform like Pinterest, which transports people into a curated experience based on their own selected preferences and interests, is not only entertaining, it's also influencing customers' purchasing behavior, especially in areas like fashion, which are so inherently personal and visual. We believe that it's a sense of discovery that compels ModCloth's customer to participate in Pinterest, and that's the same motivation that compels her to shop with us. It's essential for brands today to inspire their customers—and today there are few platforms better at doing this than Pinterest!

Pinterest Power is the ultimate guide for any small business owner hoping to leverage the Pinterest social platform to increase sales and brand awareness. Jason Miles and Karen Lacey answer the right questions for the busy entrepreneur or marketing leader looking to explore a Pinterest account for his or her business. The book details the most important aspects of launching a Pinterest strategy: basics of the platform, real-world examples from innovative brands, and strategic advice from experts in the field. There are powerful case studies from small companies such as Liberty Jane Clothing and BurdaStyle, the former seeing sales double after implementing a Pinterest strategy and the latter seeing the site refer over 25 percent of its traffic! The early adopters highlighted in the book offer invaluable best practices that will provide a solid foundation for building your own Pinterest presence.

ModCloth empowers women who love to express themselves through fashion and decor, and Pinterest empowers people who want to express themselves through visuals. I like to think we're both connecting people with the beauty that surrounds them. Clothing, food, travel, design—these are the ways we like to express who we are. The inspiration we collect along the way from our friends, families, and networks defines who we are as a community. With Pinterest, that community has no boundaries.

—*Susan Gregg Koger*
Cofounder and Chief Creative Officer at ModCloth

Acknowledgments

This project has been a gift from God, and I am grateful for his kindness toward me. I'm also grateful for the wisdom, guidance, and support of our incredible agent, Marilyn Allen. Your support is a blessing in our lives. Special thanks to my coauthor, Karen, who welcomed me into this project and wrote tirelessly to make this book the best it could be. Thank you for giving me the opportunity to work with you. This book would not have been possible without the generosity of the Pinterest team. We are incredibly grateful for your amazing product and also your willingness to contribute to the book. Without the participation of the individuals and companies we featured in the book, it would not have been nearly as cool. We are grateful for you. Finally, I'd like to acknowledge the love of my life, the amazingly talented Cinnamon Miles.

—Jason Miles

First and foremost, thank you to my agent, Marilyn Allen, for once again turning a dream into a reality. Thank you to my most amazing and talented coauthor, Jason. What an incredible marketer you are! Thank you also to Donya Dickerson for your editorial wisdom, and to Janice Race and Judy Duguid for your eagle-eye copyediting. And finally, thank you to those talented Pinterest trailblazers we interviewed for this book. You all are incredible, and I hope every reader of this book follows you and becomes a loyal, referral-generating client. Thank you for sharing your wisdom and experience.

—Karen Lacey

Introduction

*P*interest is the fastest-growing website in the history of the Internet, faster than Facebook, YouTube, or Twitter. And it's still the early days in the Pinterest epoch. As a marketer, you can't afford to ignore this amazing new platform. Already, businesses of every size are increasing referral traffic, sales, and customer satisfaction through their Pinterest presence.

You may wonder how you'll ever have time for yet one more social media platform. After reading this book you'll realize you'll actually save time by tapping into the incredible phenomenon of repinning. You'll read examples of successful Pinterest users who are seeing tens of thousands of new visits to their website, all the result of a careful, market-oriented pinning strategy. And the majority of this new traffic is based on the effects of other people pinning images from their website onto Pinterest—and from the effects of those images being repinned within Pinterest.

Pinterest is such a powerful referral generator for websites and blogs that already it's outproducing all but the largest social media outlets. Yet in comparison with those sites, it has a tiny user base. What will happen when it has hundreds of millions of members, as is forecasted? In *Pinterest Power* we walk you through how to take advantage of this Internet wonder and shorten your learning curve. Chances are, your business is benefiting from Pinterest without your even realizing it. When you actively take part in helping your fans and followers spread the word through Pinterest, it'll be like adding fuel to the fire.

Let's look at 10 concrete reasons why you should market your business using Pinterest.

10 Reasons to Market Your Business with Pinterest

1. Pinterest takes advantage of the new way of discovery on the Internet—*visually*, through friends and trusted resources rather than impersonal search engines. It's this very ingredient that has helped propel Pinterest to such early success.

2. You will connect with massive new pools of prospective clients who are visually oriented and whom you may never have been able to connect with otherwise. Keeping Pinterest's growth record in mind, you can see that this is becoming a very large pool indeed.

3. Your Pinterest content keeps working for you months after you've posted it. Unlike Facebook, Twitter, or blogs, your content is passively managed. You don't have to keep making posts and tweets to stay in front of your prospective clients. Over 80 percent of all pins are repins; this means your followers and their followers and their followers do your marketing for you.

4. Pinterest is like a giant display ad system, but all for free. You can use long, scrolling infographics if you like, or short and snappy ones. And you can average several times more click-throughs than normal Google display ads. All for free!

5. Stay-at-home moms, sole proprietors, and other small-business owners are achieving remarkable success by leveraging the power of Pinterest. The combination of being visual, having a long shelf life for content, and having an active DIY, crafts, fashion, and lifestyle user base makes this fit a natural.

6. Very low overhead is required to maintain a Pinterest presence. Yes, it takes time to get set up properly and then to keep the pinning maintained. But you don't have to worry about continually responding to posts or tweets and keeping this same start-up level of commitment. You can grow at your own pace, and those repins just keep coming through!

7. Your content is spread through new communities and groups of potential clients without your even knowing it. Because of the re-pinning feature, your ideas, solutions, products, and inspiration embark on journeys of their own once they've been pinned. Don't underestimate the power of the repin.

8. It's easy to get started even if you know very little about technology and don't like bringing attention to yourself. If your tendency is to sit back and watch but not to start your own blog or actively tweet or post on Facebook, you can quietly grow an active and effective Pinterest referral generator while still avoiding the limelight.

9. You turn your followers into gospel-spreading mavens. As opposed to those people described in reason eight above, some people are natural marketers and will utilize this in-born talent on your behalf. You can morph clients into advocates who proactively promote your products and services within their own networks.

10. You can tap into niches you never thought existed. Due to the ease and visual nature of Pinterest, there's something for everyone here, and the participants share images and follow one another. Becoming an active member of your unique niche is possible and profitable.

In *Pinterest Power* we'll show you how to achieve each one of these marketing advantages. By following our proven and Pinterest-specific techniques, tactics, and campaigns, you'll be riding the wave of the social media future.

How This Book Works

Although you can skip around and read chapters of your choosing independent of their order, the best way to get the most out of this book is simply to pick it up and read it from beginning to end. Pinterest is such a new phenomenon that you'll be benefiting from other people's learning curves in all areas.

We've broken down the book into five parts. Throughout each we sprinkle Traffic Tips—strategies for getting more traffic to your site—and quotes and anecdotes from successful Pinterest users.

Part 1, "The Power of Pinterest," gets you up and running on Pinterest and then provides a background of the site and its cofounder Ben Silbermann. You'll also hear from top Pinterest users about how they are capitalizing on the power of Pinterest. We'll finish with Jason's personal story of building his own company through social media.

Next, in Part 2, "Pinterest for Marketers," we'll reveal basic marketing techniques and explain how to start your Pinterest experience off in the most effective way.

Part 3, "Leveraging the Power of Pinterest," takes the basics you've learned and shows you how to get real, long-lasting growth from Pinterest. We'll explain how to expand into other social media markets, how to use contests to activate your followers and clients, and how to develop pins with punch that will drive your Pinterest traffic to new levels. We finish with three real-life examples of bloggers using Pinterest successfully.

Part 4, "Pinterest Selling Strategies," shows you how to integrate Pinterest within e-commerce sites, like eBay, Etsy, and Amazon. You'll learn how to feed the marketing cycle so that each avenue of sales fuels the next. We also cover different monetization strategies so that you can achieve a high level of revenue stability in line with increased growth. We finish this part with ideas for developing and launching Pinterest marketing campaigns and building the all-important e-mail address list.

The final part, "No Product? No Problem," reveals the world of Pinterest in the context of helping nonprofit organizations and communities expand their reach and participation levels. We finish with an entire chapter on Pinterest-specific resources to help you leverage the website as is.

When you've finished this book, you will truly be a Pinterest marketing professional. If you incorporate the techniques within, your success will be rapid and sustained and will be tailored to your unique business and personality.

Please note that in many cases we've blurred the faces of Pinterest users in the book's screenshots. This is a reflection of our desire to preserve their privacy and is not what you'll be seeing when you get online with Pinterest. There the images are crisp and clear.

Bonus Material

As if all that isn't enough, we provide the following four sets of bonus material on our website, http://www.PinterestPower.com.

- **10-Part Video Guide.** To access a complete 10-part companion video series to the book, simply visit http://www.pinterestpower .com. Follow along as Jason walks you through the book's chapters, shares in-depth examples, and answers common questions.

- **The in-depth interviews.** To access the complete transcripts of our interviews with Pinterest, ModCloth, Burdastyle, and the rest of the companies and individuals featured in this book, simply visit http://www.pinterestpower.com.

- **Extended resources.** To access a constantly updated list of Pinterest-related resources, visit http://www.pinterestpower.com. Check out tools, resources, and services to help you fully leverage Pinterest.

- **Bonus chapter.** To access an in-depth bonus chapter, "Launch a Small Business on Pinterest," visit http://www.pinterestpower .com. Are you ready to start a small business? Jason works with over 600 work-from-home small-business owners, and in this special chapter he shares insights and tips on how they use Pinterest to go from concept to cash.

THE POWER
OF PINTEREST

The Astounding Interest in Pinterest

*I*n the world of social media, a new star is on the horizon, capturing the imagination of millions. Pinterest.com is connecting us like never before. Its clever, ubervisual approach has propelled it into the fastest-growing website in the history of the Internet—faster even than Facebook, YouTube, or Twitter. Whereas it took Facebook 16 months to go from 50,000 to 17 million unique monthly visitors, and Twitter 22, Pinterest achieved this remarkable feat in only 9 months.

In the two years since Pinterest was launched, the phenomenon of "pinning" images onto virtual pinboards (the basic function on Pinterest) has gone viral. Pinterest has quickly captured the full spectrum of users from first-adopter teenagers to national outlets, such as *Better Homes and Gardens, Vogue*, Martha Stewart, and even the Smithsonian Institution. *Real Simple* recently became the first print magazine to top 100,000 Pinterest followers, attracted by its pinned images of recipes, childcare advice, and do-it-yourself (DIY) home improvement tips (see Figure 1.1).

In March 2012, Pinterest became the third largest social media network in the world, trailing only Twitter and Facebook. It had 18.7 million registered users and over 100 million visitors in March alone. To

Figure 1.1 *Real Simple* on Pinterest. The women's print magazine was the first to cross the 100,000-followers mark.

put it into perspective, in the same month, LinkedIn had 86 million visits, Twitter 182 million, and the granddaddy of them all, Facebook, had a whopping 7 billion. When Pinterest's numbers are extrapolated, based on conservative estimates, it's easy to see Pinterest realizing over a hundred million registered users in the next few years.

What's in a Pin?

The Pinterest difference is that it's a site about visual discovery. Each time you log in, you're greeted by other users' pinboards filled with alluring images of gardening, food, fashion, home improvement, and crafts, rather than the traditional postings and text that you might see on Facebook. Its very visualness is what's striking and has led users to admit to an unusual dichotomy—they're relaxed by the Pinterest experience, but also inspired.

This is a key factor in what keeps users coming back for more. In the company's own words, "Pinterest allows you to organize and share all the beautiful things you find on the web."

The process of pinning images is fast and easy. Pins can be created from any website the user visits. When you see an image you like, a few clicks of the mouse is all it takes to pin it onto one of your pinboards. The image retains the link to the original website, and so anyone who views the pin can go to that website and purchase or learn more about the item.

This link to the original source is an interesting aspect of the Pinterest success story. A natural sales process is created that is both quick and intuitive. Sole proprietors, small-business owners, and major corporations alike are finding that Pinterest is a great way to make money.

Gayle Butler, editor-in-chief of the magazine *Better Homes and Gardens*, said this about the economic potential in Pinterest:

> As a visual brand where images and ideas are so central to what we do, we are extremely excited about Pinterest. This is a tremendous complement.

Recent data show that more referral traffic is driven from Pinterest back to the sellers' websites than Google+, LinkedIn, and YouTube *combined*. Members are tapping into massive new pools of potential customers, who are actively visiting their websites and blogs in return. Pinterest is no here-one-day-gone-the-next social media starlet. It's hip and hot, and it's altering the landscape of social media forever.

How People Are Benefiting from Pinterest

Basically, Pinterest is a place to share images of things you love. It's social because your friends (and potential customers) can see what you're up to, make comments, and share their own images. But you will also receive comments, repins, and ideas from users across the world.

This social media model makes it incredibly efficient as a place to store and sort your ideas. Let's say you want to remodel your kitchen. You can build a "Kitchen Remodeling" pinboard filled with ideas that you might otherwise lose or forget. Rather than having a file folder bulging with ripped-out magazine pages, you have a neat and tidy set of virtual pinboards. As you surf the web for ideas, you pin the ones you like.

As well, you can easily search other Pinterest users' kitchen remodeling ideas and repin them onto your own boards. In this process you're tapping into thousands of ideas, presorted and categorized for you. Search for kitchen sinks, tiles, light fixtures, stove tops, and whatever else specifically interests you. The pinboard format makes the process entertaining and just plain great to look at.

Maybe you're planning a wedding. You can create one board filled with wedding dress designs, another with cake pictures, and yet one more with flower and table arrangements. Not only is it a place to display and sort your ideas, but your friends and family can see and comment on what you're thinking.

Folks who are always on the hunt for a new recipe or craft idea love Pinterest. They're having a dinner party and need vegetarian appetizers, gluten-free desserts, or new ways to cook that same ol' chicken breast.

But the boundaries of Pinterest don't end in the land-of-everyday. One user, Susan, pins about women in planetary science. Another Pinterest user has a pinboard filled with nothing but bizarre and detailed maps of the world. Clearly, the only limits are within your own imagination. Pinterest supports it all through pinning, repinning, liking, and commenting.

As we were writing this book in May 2012, we had a chance to ask the members of the Pinterest team to share exclusive insights with us for marketers and small-business owners. We'll share their responses throughout the book. (To read the entire interview, along with the transcripts of other companies we interviewed, visit http://www.Pinterestpower.com.) Here is what they had to say about using Pinterest for marketing:

Q. Pinterest has seen phenomenal growth, and many marketers are evaluating how best to use the site. Is there a specific message or word of encouragement you'd like to share with them as they prepare to bring marketing campaigns to life on Pinterest?

A. Pinterest lets people organize and share the things they love, including their inspirations or concrete ideas for many offline activities and events. We think there are a lot of opportunities to learn more about what people are searching for or interested in, and it's an exciting time for brands to dip in and familiarize themselves with the new dynamics of discovery, sharing, and self-expression we're trying to build.

Pinterest and Your Small Business

Within this ever-increasing whirlwind of pinning and repinning, Pinterest has become an exceptional tool for increasing e-commerce sales. Because the images are easy to pin and they link back to the original websites, Pinterest is a natural for businesses.

In fact, Pinterest has fast become a social media leader in generating referral traffic back to the original website from which the image was pinned. Pinterest and e-commerce business have evolved into a natural fit.

Interestingly, many business owners have found increased referral traffic from Pinterest without even having a Pinterest profile. Pinterest users find their images and pin them on their boards, and then the images are repinned again and again. Each time the image is pinned or repinned, a link to the business owner's website is created.

This is the experience of one of the coauthors of the book, Jason: An example of the magic of pinning and repinning is from an online company called Liberty Jane Clothing, founded and run by my wife, Cinnamon, and me. On our company's Pinterest pinboards we've made a total of 487 pins; yet those images have been repinned 8,349 times. Many of those images have links directly back to Liberty Jane Clothing's website, which means an enormous increase in referral traffic. In fact, the first month we actively used Pinterest our sales doubled! This is just the tip of the iceberg when it comes to the power of Pinterest.

Yet one more intriguing feature for small businesses is the longevity built into the pinning process. Twenty-nine weeks after a single Liberty Jane Clothing image was pinned, it was *still* generating referral traffic to our website. We didn't even pin it up in the first place. Now that's powerful.

Here's How It Works

The best way to understand the Pinterest difference is to experience it yourself. We will cover many more basic functions in Chapter 5, but this will get you up and running.

1. Joining Pinterest

Go to http://www.pinterest.com. The process couldn't be easier. While previously you had to go through an invitation-only system, now you simply click on Join Pinterest and follow along step-by-step (see Figure 1.2). If you already belong, this is where you will click on Login to bring up your personalized Pinterest boards and people you follow. You don't need to join to have a look at Pinterest and see if it's for you, but chances are you'll want to start building your own boards and collecting those things you find inspiring and interesting.

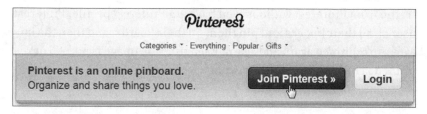

Figure 1.2 Joining Pinterest is quick and easy.

Currently, you must sign up through your Facebook or Twitter account. If you have business accounts in either of these, be sure to sign up through it rather than your personal account. Then be sure to pick the Facebook or Twitter business account that has the most followers or potential. You will get the fans associated with that account automatically loaded onto the Pinterest system, and therefore they'll be easy to invite to join and follow you. By picking the right list to begin with, you'll save an enormous amount of time.

2. Following and Unfollowing

The pins from the people you follow will make up the content of the site and therefore the quality of your Pinterest experience. During the registration process, you will be asked to choose from a diverse list of interests, such as women's and men's apparel, home decor, education, travel, pets, and the like.

When you first see your Pinterest home page, Pinterest will have selected people for you to follow based on your registration responses.

The images these people pin will be what you see each time you log in to Pinterest.

It's important to edit these and develop your own set of people to follow. In this way you tailor your experience to those areas that interest you the most.

A great place to find new people to follow is to access friends from Facebook and Twitter. On any Pinterest page, hover your cursor over your name in the upper right-hand corner and then click on Find Friends. From here you will be able to follow any friends who are current Pinterest users. (See Figure 1.3.) You can also invite non-Pinterest friends to join.

Figure 1.3 Follow friends of yours who are current Pinterest users.

Another way to find people to follow is to type in the keyword of an interest of yours in the search box in the top left-hand corner of any Pinterest page. If cooking is your thing, type in recipe names to get you started, like *apple pies, BBQ, vegan,* or *chicken saltimbocca.* You'll be amazed at the images and creativity that come up (see Figure 1.4).

Figure 1.4 This mouth-watering selection of images and recipes came up by doing a keyword search for *chicken saltimbocca*.

To follow someone, click on the image and then on the big red Follow button. To unfollow someone, click on the image and then on the Unfollow button. It couldn't be easier.

3. Building Your Pinboards

Building pinboards is actually optional. You can explore and enjoy Pinterest without ever creating one. But if you want to get the full experience as well as reap the small-business benefits of Pinterest, it's time to roll up your sleeves.

You will be directed to build your pinboards in the registration process. But you can also build and edit them at any other time. To do this, in the top right-hand corner of any Pinterest page, click on Add+. From the pop-up box, click on Create a Board.

Give your board a name, file it under a category, and then click on Create Board. How easy is that?

To access your boards, click on your name in the upper right-hand corner of any Pinterest page. We'll go into the nuances and strategies of what types of boards to build in Chapter 5.

4. Understanding the Basics of Pinning and Repinning

The easiest way to pin is to first download the Pin It feature that Pinterest provides (see Figure 1.5). Again, you will be directed to do this in the registration process. If you don't do it then, you can, as noted earlier, do it another time. You simply hover your cursor over the About button in the upper right-hand corner of any Pinterest page. Then click on the Pin It button. You will find instructions that will walk you through the process of installing the Pin It button into the bookmark toolbar of your web browser. You can also download an iPhone Pin It app.

Figure 1.5 Install the Pin It button on your bookmark toolbar for fast and easy pinning.

Let's say you found a recipe for a smoked salmon appetizer you'd like to post on your Favorite Foods pinboard. Bring up the web page with the image you want to pin. Then click on the Pin It button in your book-mark toolbar.

TRAFFIC TIP

Always pin an image (as opposed to a repin) from the orig-inal source rather than from a Google image or an e-mail. This way the original link to the website is included with the image when it's pinned and repinned. By doing this, the en-tire Pinterest community is helped, since anyone can click on the image and go directly to the source for more informa-tion. If you're not sure if you've done it right, just click on the final pinned image and see where it takes you.

After you click on the Pin It button, all the images on that web page will appear. Hover your mouse over the image you want to pin, and a Pin This button will appear (see Figure 1.6).

Figure 1.6 Click the Pin This button to pin your image onto your pinboard.

Click this button, and you'll be asked to describe your pin and which board you want to pin it on. Click Pin It and you're done! (See Figure 1.7.)

Figure 1.7 Pick a pinboard for your image and give it a brief description before you click the final Pin It button.

To repin an image from someone else's pinboard onto your own, hover your mouse over the image and you will be given the choices to repin, like, or comment. It's as easy as that! (See Figure 1.8.)

Figure 1.8 Hover your mouse over any image to repin it.

Repinning is so easy and intuitive that it's become the most common activity on Pinterest. In fact, within two hours of posting the smoked salmon appetizer image shown in Figures 1.6 and 1.7, it had been repinned over 40 times. As you will see, this is very good news for those wanting to increase sales while using Pinterest.

5. Following Pin Etiquette

As with any public venue, proper etiquette is crucial for an overall positive experience. The Golden Rule applies. Always be polite. Don't post objectionable content, and if you see it on someone's pinboard, report it to Pinterest. It's up to us all to maintain the quality of the community.

As well, use a soft sell. Yes, you can use Pinterest to increase business sales, and we'll show you exactly how to do that throughout this book. But none of us like to be hard pitched or feel like we're being used. Give more than you receive.

6. Taking Time to Explore!

Go ahead and get involved in the Pinterest community. Spend some time exploring what people are posting and commenting on. One great way to do this is to search by category.

Click on the central Pinterest icon to get back to your main page. Beneath this icon you have five choices you can navigate: Pinners you follow, Everything, Videos, Popular, and Gifts.

Hover your mouse over Everything to bring up the list of categories. From here, click on whatever category strikes your fancy and have fun! You'll be amazed at what you turn up. Images and ideas will inspire you to repin images onto your own boards in no time.

This is the magic of Pinterest. Users have a place to express themselves and what they love. And the experience has only just begun.

What's Next?

In the next chapter we'll have a look at three supermodels—three small businesses that are using Pinterest to dramatically increase site traffic, sales, and brand impact. The formula isn't rocket science; it's just the power of Pinterest. Read on!

Supermodels

*I*ndividuals and businesses benefit from Pinterest in unique and creative ways. Therefore, throughout this book you'll read the stories of successful people who've unlocked the secrets to this powerful form of social media. It's important to understand the theories behind marketing strategies and techniques, but hearing someone's own real story helps us turn that theory into reality. We learn how these people make Pinterest work within the everyday world of competition, and how Pinterest helps them navigate the changing needs of customers and the shifting dynamics of technology. From this combination of solid concepts and their practical application, we can structure our own marketing strategies and campaigns that suit our unique situations and personalities.

In this chapter we tell the stories of three Pinterest supermodels. Not the runway type—rather those businesses that have achieved success and are working the Pinterest advantage to take them to the next level. You'll read about ModCloth, an online retailer of indie fashion and decor; BurdaStyle, the largest online DIY fashion and sewing community; and Lil Blue Boo, a popular blog founded by Ashley Hackshaw encouraging people to find their creative streak.

Success begets success, and this is your chance to listen to some of the pros. Apply what fits to your situation, stash away ideas for the future, and "think big, start small."

ModCloth

ModCloth.com is an innovative online retailer specializing in clothing and decor from over 700 independent designers and suppliers. Items are carefully selected from all over the world by cofounder Susan Gregg Koger and the ModCloth buying team, and customers then purchase directly from the ModCloth website. ModCloth's mission is to democratize the fashion industry and change the way clothing is produced, sold, and even marketed by empowering independent designers, style bloggers, and their own community.

While ModCloth had an active and successful social media presence already, when Pinterest came on the scene, it quickly caught the eye of the company's marketing folks, mainly because of the way it arrived.

ModCloth explains, "Our fans brought Pinterest to our attention. We first noticed it due to the amount of traffic coming from Pinterest to ModCloth.com. It's a platform that our core demographic loves. According to Pinterest, their users are 85 percent female and the largest age demographic is 18–34 years old. Also, we found that the type of content that resonates on Pinterest is also the type of editorial content that we generate on our blog, such as DIY, fashion, and food. We had a great demographic and psychographic match!"

Because current clients were already pinning ModCloth images onto Pinterest and because the core message of ModCloth was so similar to the expectations of the typical Pinterest user, ModCloth decided to take on this new social media platform and become an active member of the Pinterest community. In the fall of 2011, the company opened its Pinterest account, and its current fan base fueled an exponential rise in the number of followers.

Figure 2.1 shows ModCloth's "Vintage Vantage" pinboard, featuring stylish, retro images of fashion, the times, and movie stars. With over 40,000 followers, this board appeals to a huge potential client base. The company has filled other boards with ideas, tips, and cool designs, and there is even a "Guest Pinner Gallery" board where followers can contribute images of what they love.

In short, ModCloth has become a valuable go-to source on Pinterest for hip fashion and decor. This in turn has stimulated an enormous increase in referral traffic back to ModCloth's main site. The company notes, "Pinterest competes with Facebook as one of our top unpaid

Figure 2.1 ModCloth's "Vintage Vantage" pinboard is filled with fun and inspiring images from the past.

referral sites as far as traffic and revenue. As Pinterest climbed the ranks in our referral sources, we saw its intrinsic value as a traffic generating tool.

"Last week [early April 2012], a customer said that they loved seeing ModCloth get so much attention on Pinterest but was disappointed those products were now quickly selling out. Since we launched our Pinterest brand page we've seen traffic from the site grow by 1000%. In the last thirty days alone, we've had 140,000 items pinned from our site, which amplified to 270,000 repins (data from Curalate)."

TRAFFIC TIP

When you launch your brand on Pinterest, consider making an integrated campaign out of it where you simultaneously use all your existing channels to promote your presence. Let your fans, followers, and clients know they can now find you on this hip new site they've just been reading about. If nothing else, they'll visit you on Pinterest out of curiosity—and then stay out of fascination.

These incredible numbers ModCloth has achieved resulted from a combination of different marketing strategies. And one of these is contests.

ModCloth Contests

In early 2012, ModCloth held its first Pinterest contest called "Something ModCloth, Something You." Followers created a wedding inspiration board that included ModCloth products. The company then chose a winner, who received a gift card along with the recognition that came with having her inspiration board turned into stylebook images. For a first contest, the company achieved pretty considerable results. (To learn more about creating your own Pinterest contest, see Chapter 9.)

The company says, "The quantifiable results from the contest were participation, new followers, increased traffic from Pinterest, and customer sentiment. Through the contest, we gained thousands of new followers and had a total of 600 entries. The new followers were a mix of existing customers on Pinterest, customers we introduced to Pinterest, and new customers who discovered us through the contest. Since more ModCloth items were being pinned and repinned, we also saw a bump in referral traffic from Pinterest. Overall, our customers loved the contest and the fact we were so engaged with this platform."

In short, ModCloth discovered that contests on Pinterest rock. The company's advice for running your first contest is, "When creating a contest for any social media platform, it's important to understand the natural behavior of the site's members. We intuitively saw that weddings and inspirational wedding boards resonated with the Pinterest audience, so we chose to reward that behavior in the context of ModCloth."

Best Practices

Below are several best practices ModCloth discovered when using Pinterest:

- Make sure it's easy for your fans to extract images from your website onto Pinterest. ModCloth has added a Pin It button to each product page and on the ModCloth blog as well.

- Always use the best images you can find or create. In order to motivate your users to share these images, they have to be appealing.

- By making your Pinterest presence clear on your website, your users will be encouraged to share those images on Pinterest. It also keeps you in their minds when they participate on Pinterest.

- Measure your results through various third-party analytical tools designed to track Pinterest traffic. These include Pintics, Pinpuff (similar to Klout), Pinerly, Pinreach, Pinfluencer, and Curalate. (For more on these, see Chapter 19.)

- When conducting contests, ModCloth prefers to let users submit their contest boards publicly to increase the exposure and excitement.

ModCloth is a successful company furthering its growth through marketing with Pinterest. The company took advantage of this new form of social media and is witnessing an increase in referral traffic, customer happiness, and revenue.

The company says, "Due to the rise of visual discovery, highly pinnable products on site, and a demographic that loves social media, we have the perfect recipe for Pinterest success."

BurdaStyle

BurdaStyle is the largest online DIY fashion and sewing community, with over three-quarters of a million registered members. Its aim is to bring the craft of sewing to a new generation of fashion designers, hobbyists, and DIYers, as well as inspire fashion enthusiasts. The website houses literally thousands of stylish handcrafted clothes, downloadable PDF sewing patterns, tutorials, and project ideas, and it supports a community passionate about sewing and fashion.

It is also an avid Pinterest user. In BurdaStyle's words, "We've been using Pinterest for over a year now [since early 2011] and are continuing to explore the site and adjust our use to increase its value for business. We study who's liking our pins, which pins are being liked and repinned, and even what time of day our pins get the most attention. Overall we've seen a significant increase in BurdaStyle activity on Pinterest as well as an increase in site referrals."

Given that BurdaStyle became active with Pinterest at such an early stage in Pinterest's history, it had to pioneer its way through various learning curves. Fortunately for us, we can benefit from its trial and error:

"During our first experiences on the site, we were pinning as frantically as we felt. Once we slowed down and became more selective with our pinning, we found an increase in attention. We began to realize where our Pinterest audience's interests lay and began to more carefully curate our boards based on these interests. We focused on quality and the personality of our brand."

BurdaStyle notes, "Pinterest allows us to collect and share what inspires by simply pinning images. A well-curated board can be nothing less than exciting. So do just that—pin what excites you."

It's this very line of thinking that creates more and more followers. When people log in to Pinterest, they are swept away by beautiful images of places, foods, fashion, and even humor. The images are so intriguing and alluring, it may take people awhile to remember why they logged on in the first place! (See Figure 2.2.)

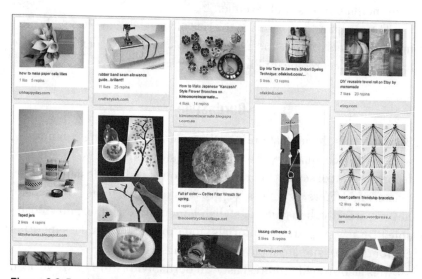

Figure 2.2 BurdaStyle's "DIY and Craft Projects" board is filled with creative and colorful ideas and solutions.

In all, between April 2011 and April 2012, Pinterest became one of BurdaStyle's strongest social media networks. Not bad for a first year!

Lil Blue Boo

Founded in 2009 by Ashley Hackshaw, Lil Blue Boo is a blog (http://www.lilblueboo.com) all about encouraging others to find their creative streak. What began as a place for Ashley to share craft projects with friends and family quickly grew into a popular blog covering DIY, lifestyle, sewing patterns, and clothing lines, and more recently it became a community forum.

In Ashley's words, "At first Pinterest was just a source of inspiration and ideas. The first board I created was a style wish list of clothing. Then I began to pin my own DIY ideas and the repinning started to take off. Pinterest began driving a large amount of traffic to my website."

Ashley continued to experiment with Pinterest and watched the referral traffic grow. In hindsight she wished she would have anticipated the wide variety of boards she would need from the very beginning. As some folks only follow specific boards, she might have missed those who would have found her newer boards more interesting. And as you may very well have experienced already, it's easy to get wrapped up in the beautiful photos on Pinterest. However, the most popular items are repinned over and over. So she believes it's a good idea to limit your time on Pinterest so your own ideas stay fresh and intriguing. (See Figure 2.3.)

Despite these learning curves, Ashley's success is astounding. To date she gets about 20,000 unique visitors a month to her blog from Pinterest and approximately 100,000 related page views. As well, she's had over 31,000 repins. That means over 31,000 times other people have helped her do her marketing for her!

Best Practices

Below are several of Ashley's best practices regarding marketing on Pinterest:

- Share favorite images with Facebook fans; this practice has helped boost her Pinterest traffic, even if the images aren't business related.

Figure 2.3 Lil Blue Boo is a successful creativity blog founded and run by Ashley Hackshaw.

- Understand which are your most popular pins and which get pinned the most times from your website. This will show you what kind of information appeals most to readers and which posts you should be promoting more.

- Make sure to pin your images directly from the blog posting, not the general blog URL. This way your viewer doesn't have to go searching through the entire post history.

- Analyze which pinboards people are following, and then pin more to those boards. Reward your followers.

- Pay attention not only to the images, but to the titles too. Ashley creates photo collages from her blog with catchy titles. These become the images most likely to be pinned, and they're visually appealing on Pinterest.

- Categorize your items well right from the beginning.

■ Look elsewhere for inspiration beside Pinterest. This will help keep your ideas fresh.

Ashley is a great supermodel to learn from. Visit her blog, and follow her on Pinterest. Her success just keeps growing. "Just this year to date [May 2012]," she says, "traffic from other people pinning my page has resulted in over 17,000 visitors to my Glowstick Lanterns and 13,000 visitors to my Vintage Sign tutorial. Those two went viral, and I'm not sure how many times they've been repinned."

We can imagine they've been repinned many times indeed!

A New Way of Networking

The story of Pinterest and its cofounding CEO Ben Silbermann spans a childhood passion for bugs all the way to the sink-or-swim world of Silicon Valley start-ups. Ben's path reveals for us not only what the roots are of this newest Internet phenomenon, but also why its core structure makes it so attractive to small-business owners. By peering into the Pinterest story, we're able to see why this social media site taps a nerve so deep within its users. We learn how this unique process of self-expression has set the foundation for a new way of networking.

The story of Pinterest is also the story of entrepreneurship. If you're a small-business owner, or want to be one, then this is your story too. Each start-up business, whether selling crafts from your home or designing one of the largest social media networks in the world, has many of the same struggles and goals—just in different proportions. We can all learn from success stories of any magnitude.

Yet this isn't just a how-one-person-beat-the-odds tale. The very nature of this new form of discovery—a visual discovery via friends and family—means delving deep into human emotions and passions. It means a format for self-expression like none other, all of which is integral to the power of Pinterest. Within this new form of discovery lies one of the greatest benefits to the small-business owner: an astounding increase in the quantity and quality of referral traffic to your website.

We'll show you how.

The Birth of a Dream—Ben Silbermann's Story

The story of Ben Silbermann and the founding of Pinterest demonstrates three key tenets of entrepreneurship that anyone can use to grow a business with Pinterest. Dreams will differ, but key lessons can be mined and applied to speed the process of success.

Ben's story begins with a childhood fascination with collecting things, especially bugs. Born and raised in Des Moines, Iowa, to parents who were both doctors, Ben spent his early years catching, collecting, and categorizing hundreds of insects and other creepy crawlies. Spiders, beetles, centipedes, you name it; he pinned them on boards and carefully labeled each one. This instinct to preserve and display what he found interesting would later blossom into the core idea of Pinterest.

Up until his junior year at Yale, Ben had assumed he would follow the family tradition and become a doctor. However, he realized this wasn't where his passion lay and was left wondering what new goal he could follow. What kind of work could he do that would provide for a family but also give him a sense of meaning and purpose in life? So he did what many of us do when we're searching for that perfect niche—we try a whole lot of different things.

He majored in political science, studied business, and became fascinated with the web and the possibilities within. After a stint consulting in Washington, D.C., where he met his future wife, they packed their bags and flew west to Silicon Valley, the modern-day mecca of entrepreneurship. From here he scored a job with Google, and this, in combination with the paradigm-shifting culture of the valley, changed his world.

At Google the concept of a crazy idea just plain didn't exist. If you thought up something outlandish, people didn't roll their eyes and snicker; rather, they booted up their laptops and broke the idea down into actionable steps. Anything became possible. This seismic shift in thought process left a deep impression on Ben. So much so that with his wife's prodding, two years later he left Google with no plan in place—just a dream to build his own company.

Dream Building 101

Three key lessons can be distilled from Ben's convoluted journey toward Pinterest.

Lesson One. Follow Your Passion

This, Ben certainly did. He took his passion for collecting, and with two friends and eventual cofounders of Pinterest, Evan Sharp and Paul Sciarra, began designing a site that would allow users to express their interests through virtual pinboards. What he discovered by following his passion became the premise for Pinterest—a place for people to express themselves.

Ben's thought was that most people understand the notion of collections. All you need to do to see what people are interested in is to walk through their home: what books do they read, what art is on their walls, what sense of design and color are they drawn to? These are all ways we say who we are, often without realizing that's what we're doing. We're not all movie stars or professional athletes; in fact, few of us are. Yet despite this lack of fame, we all have a deep need to express ourselves and what we love. This vein runs so deep that Ben feels three core aspects of this need for self-expression are what have made Pinterest so successful:

1. Collecting as a form of self-expression

2. Discovering new things handpicked by people we trust, not search bots

3. Being involved in a community of people that inspire one another

Ben explains:

> Most everyone is proud of some aspect of their life, whether it's the furniture in their house, or it's the clothes they wear every day. We wanted to build a site that celebrated that. That's the very first thing we wanted to do.

The founding trio wanted users of the site to be able to express and share their passions. In a typical search engine like Yahoo! or Google, you type in a keyword, and up comes a list of sites you can search through to find what you're looking for. You must first have an idea of what you want to find; then you're offered a list of links and an impersonal array of banner ads in the hope of garnering your interest.

They wanted something different. Their vision was to allow people to find inspiration and ideas through other people, not search engines. As Ben sums up:

> Let's let people express themselves in a way that is true and authentic to who they are. And let's let people discover things not through any other means than through their friends and other people.

Lesson Two. Think Big, Start Small, Be Patient!

Four months from its launch, Pinterest had only 200 users, and this despite Ben, Evan, and Paul inviting all their friends and family to join. People weren't catching on to the idea. However, Ben and his team didn't give up or change their direction, but instead they focused on refining their website. The vision remained in place, and they diligently worked on making the experience the best one possible.

For the first couple of years, Pinterest experienced the same steady growth rate—40 to 50 percent or more per month. Those 200 users in the first quarter of 2010 quickly grew to over 11 million unique visitors in January 2011. In March 2012, Pinterest became the third largest social media website in the world and is still growing fast. When these growth rates are extrapolated, it's easy to see that Pinterest will soon have well over 100 million members. It pays to be patient and stick to your vision.

What caused the rapid growth is a concept called *virality*—meaning that which causes something to go viral. It works this way: each user or viewer shares what he or she used or viewed with more than one person, who in turn shares with more than one person, and so on. Eventually outstanding growth is achieved, and this happened at Pinterest in a very big way.

Josephine Kimberling (http://www.JosephineKimberling.com and www .pinterest.com/josephine), a successful surface designer and licensing artist and avid Pinterest user, had this to say about following your passion:

> Since college I have dreamt of working for myself so that I could contribute to beautifying the world by creating artwork, design solutions, and delicious color stories from my unique point of view. I am very thankful that I get to do what I do because it's what I love, what I believe is my purpose in this world, and what I've committed 12+ years of my life to professionally cultivate. I believe it's important to follow your heart and to do the best you can with the talents you have.

When building your small business with Pinterest, it will serve you well to apply the same combination of patience and vision that Ben did. The tools and techniques you will learn in this book work, but the benefits take time to accumulate. Follow your passion; then stay true to that vision and work on refining it. Apply what you learn here, and watch your business grow organically, naturally, with a solid foundation, rather than on the precarious limbs of expensive advertising, a wavering sense of direction, or lack of perseverance. Remember to think big, start small, and be patient!

Lesson Three. Nurture Your Relationships

In other words, let those who understand your vision come to you. Then serve them better than they've ever been served before.

"Midwestern moms and Mormons." This is how Pinterest's first users have been described. Do you really think these were the target markets Ben had in mind? Not likely, but he certainly didn't say no. It turned out that a group of Ben's childhood friends in Iowa caught on to the magic of Pinterest, as did a group of designers in Utah he'd given a talk to early on. Ben could have pushed and shoved trying to get a more classic target market going, but instead he saw who Pinterest's users were and nurtured them like never before.

Ben sent personal e-mails to the first 5,000 Pinterest users, asking them about their experience and what he could do to improve it. That's customer service. Each of those people most probably told someone about the experience, those "someones" signed up and told other people, and the snowball kept building as it rolled right on downhill.

This experience of having two early-adopter groups that actually formed the genesis of Pinterest came as a surprise to Ben. He realized that right along with collecting as a form of expression and discovering new things handpicked by people, Pinterest provided the opportunity to belong to a community of people who inspired one another. This is what was happening in Iowa and Utah; these are the people that understood Ben's vision. In exchange, he followed dream rule number three by nurturing those relationships.

Ben learned that Pinterest has blossomed so rapidly in part because users are inspired by the experience. It's not full of impersonal algorithms that deliver results in the hope of getting you to buy something. Rather, Pinterest is full of people just like you who want to share what they love. Ben notes:

> Part of the mission of Pinterest is actually to get you off the site and inspire you to do things you otherwise wouldn't have the confidence to do.

Imagine building a website where one of the core goals is to get you offline. The concept is so appealing in this age of online addiction, that it's become one of the primary drivers. People see new ideas and creations brought to them by trusted people and then are inspired to take action and create things themselves.

As your business grows on Pinterest, you may be surprised by who's showing up to the party. Don't fight it; celebrate it. And treat your visitors like the royalty they are. These people will in turn do your marketing for you.

A New Form of Discovery

It's this concept of people discovering new things via people rather than keywords that has led to a new form of Internet discovery. We have so many things to choose from that the best way to filter through the choices is also the oldest way—find out what someone you trust is doing. We almost always trust other people's recommendations over a generic advertisement. We can read up on what the experts say is best, but at the end of the day we listen to the advice from someone we know.

Pinterest's very nature fosters this process of discovery. Users develop a network of trusted sources where they go to see what's new and exciting and to find things they might be interested in. This is what has propelled Pinterest to where it is. And it's also what will help you grow your own small business because it has created one of the key advantages to Pinterest: a dramatic increase in the quantity and quality of referral traffic to your website.

Let's look at how this works.

The Pin-nacle of Discovery—Referral Traffic

How would you like to sit back and watch qualified referrals click onto your website with little effort from you? Sounds like it's too good to be true? The facts are in, and they show that despite its short Internet life, Pinterest drives an incredible amount of referral traffic. Yet all this happens with less work involved. How could this be so?

Pinterest is a social media site by people for people; therefore referral traffic is natural because people love to talk about and share what interests them. To fully grasp how this works, you first must understand how it doesn't work. Or rather, how it works less efficiently. Let's start with a look at two of the current social media behemoths: Facebook and YouTube. Generating referral traffic from these two standard bearers is certainly possible and commonly done. The thing is, it's done better with Pinterest.

To generate a referral link from Facebook to your website, for example, you or a Facebook friend must manually post your website's link on your or your friend's wall. This takes a direct effort and isn't done that often. To create a referral link on YouTube, you will need to create a video that has a link to your website. It's labor intensive.

The problem is that the links are separate from the social interaction on these two sites. The most common functions on Facebook are to "Like," "Comment," or "Share" content, none of which creates referral links back to the user's website. YouTube's most used functions are to "Watch a Video," "Comment," or "Subscribe" to a channel. Again, no new links are created. This is the fundamental difference. On Pinterest the links are part of the social interaction.

The basic function for users of Pinterest is uploading images to save and share. When you pin an image on Pinterest, you're creating a link without even thinking about it.

But pinning is just the beginning. Approximately 80 percent of Pinterest images are actually repins. Viewers see images on someone else's pinboard and repin them onto their own. The majority of the time this happens, the referral link comes right along with it.

If you remember from Chapter 1, we talked about posting an image of a smoked salmon appetizer and within just a couple of hours the image had been repinned over 40 times. That's over 40 new referral links to the original website with no new effort. In fact, the owners of the website never even knew these links had been created but continue to benefit from any traffic they generate. Now that's powerful. And that's why Pinterest is a monster referral traffic generator.

Generating referral links isn't the only marketing benefit to Pinterest by any means. But it's a key stepping-stone to understanding many of the marketing concepts you'll learn in subsequent chapters. This is a crucial part of the foundation upon which you'll grow your small business.

The story of Ben Silbermann and Pinterest has lessons for any entrepreneur or small-business owner. But for our purposes in this book, it's important to understand that the very DNA of this website is what makes it such a natural for marketing. Pinterest is structured differently from other social media sites. You can think of it as second-generation social media, and others are already following in its virtual footsteps.

The Pinterest story is also phenomenal because it begins with a nine-year-old boy waking up in the morning excited to pin bugs onto his collection board. It ends, for now, with that same person building the fastest-growing website in the history of the Internet based on the same vision—pinning favorite things onto boards. Each dream can come true, and Ben has proved it. Yours can too.

A Personal Story

S ome of the best lessons in life come from real-life stories about how people in the trenches make their worlds work. You've seen three already with the examples of ModCloth, BurdaStyle, and Lil Blue Boo. In Chapter 11 you'll read three more stories of how successful bloggers used Pinterest with amazing results.

In this chapter you'll hear Jason's story, about how he and his wife, Cinnamon, built their own business, Liberty Jane Clothing. You'll read how they experimented with different social media platforms until one day they stumbled upon the new kid on the block, a crazy new site called Pinterest. And you'll recognize common links with what you might be experiencing with social media, e-commerce, and the rapid pace of change in technology.

Through research, experience, and those evil twins Trial and Error, Jason and Cinnamon developed over 14,000 Facebook fans and 7,600 YouTube subscribers with over 1.2 million video views. However, it wasn't until they began studying and applying the power of Pinterest that the entire formula kicked in. Within one month after they began marketing on Pinterest, they doubled their monthly referral traffic from Pinterest. Even more interesting, they did this by spending far less time and effort than they would have with traditional social media platforms.

The rest of the chapter comes from Jason's own words.

An Aspiring Eight-Year-Old

Cinnamon began sewing clothes for her 18-inch Kimberly doll when she was eight years old. Her mom taught her to sew, and it immediately became Cinnamon's passion. She loved making those outfits! She became so obsessed that she accidently sewed right into her finger. The needle had broken off in her tiny finger, and her mom had to rush her to the hospital. The next day Cinnamon told her mom she had to keep working and only needed help changing her bandage and installing a new needle in the sewing machine.

At one point Cinnamon's mom, Vicki, had worked for Switched on Ltd., a designer label in Los Angeles, and so she was an amazing sewing teacher. As well, a friend of Cinnamon's grandmother worked for Bob Mackie, a famous designer of celebrity clothing. She'd give Cinnamon scraps of fancy material that Cinnamon then used to make dresses for her dolls. They weren't perfect, but not bad at all for an eight-year-old.

After Cinnamon and I got married and started our own family, our daughters began getting into American Girl dolls. However, when Cinnamon looked beyond the American Girl catalogue, she found the outfits were low quality, designed poorly, or both. So she decided to make her own outfits for our daughters' dolls. They'd be similar to things girls see on TV and in magazines—contemporary, fun, and couture.

The Birth of a Business

Cinnamon's doll clothes came out so well that we decided maybe there was a business opportunity here. With a lot of prayer and planning, we began to put the pieces together. It was overwhelming but fun.

We decided not to become focused on high volume or manufacturing in mass quantities, but rather we would emphasize an intense level of detail, high-quality fabrics, and designs that were bold and trendy. Our goal became to translate contemporary fashion hits into the 18-inch doll market for collectors and young girls excited by today's fashions. We decided to have a line of spring and fall original designs each year.

Finally, we picked our youngest daughter's first and middle name for the brand—Liberty Jane. It sounded like a clothing brand, and so we went for it and think it works. Now our daughter is the official spokesgirl for the company.

The Journey of Liberty Jane Clothing

From February 2008 to the summer of 2009, we sold our items exclusively through eBay auctions. Our auctions became a spectacle as the prices frequently soared past the limits of what people would consider normal. Prices often ended over $100 and went as high as $153. But by the end of that summer, we were burned out. It was a lot of work. We'd met our goal of $1,000 a month, but we realized we'd reached the end of our business model.

So we went looking for new business models. We were influenced most strongly by the writing of Jim Cockrum, author of *The Silent Sales Machine Hiding Inside of eBay* and *Free Marketing 101*.

The end result was that we decided to publish Cinnamon's patterns as a new product. The reasoning was fairly simple. Although we were honored by and thrilled at the high prices our outfits got at auction, we realized there are a lot of people who won't ever pay $100 for a doll's outfit. However, they would gladly buy a pattern and try to make something themselves. Plus we wanted a scalable model—one that allowed us to sell items without physically fulfilling the orders ourselves. So we created Liberty Jane Patterns (http://www.libertyjanepatterns.com) as a way to sell patterns directly to consumers.

The first month we sold 11 patterns and gave away several hundred for free. However, the transition from eBay created a collection of benefits that fueled our business growth.

First, now we had to develop our own method for contacting customers and following up after the sale was completed. Because of this, we learned the original and still single most important online marketing practice—e-mail marketing through weekly e-mail newsletters. (See Chapter 16.)

Initially our e-mail list consisted of 120 customers. However, by learning how to leverage the power of free, as in free patterns, we began getting 500 to 600 new prospects signing up each month.

We began watching our website statistics and discovered where our customers were coming from. There were niche-specific fan boards and forums that we didn't even know existed. We started to realize that social networks, large and small, were a key to our success. Most important, we understood that we would have to generate our own traffic; we couldn't rely on eBay to send customers our way. And the best traffic was that referred by one customer to another, either through word of mouth or social sharing.

As we explored how to use social networks to expand our social engagement, we found a fantastic partner in YouTube. As it turns out, there's a thriving doll collector community hiding inside of YouTube. Who knew?

We started conducting design contests on YouTube several times a year with staggering results. Our top-performing contest had 2,400 video responses, making it one of the most responded-to videos of all time in YouTube's how-to and style category.

We also developed a strong Facebook fan page effort, as we found that strength in one social network (YouTube) led to strength in another (Facebook).

In the fall of 2011, two years after we started selling doll patterns online, our little business was experiencing some serious growth. We had over 1 million video views on YouTube with over 7,000 subscribers. We had over 12,000 newsletter subscribers and over 12,000 Facebook fans.

Although Twitter had emerged on the scene, we decided it wasn't right for us for a couple of reasons. First, we didn't have time to constantly tweet. Second, our business was visually driven, not oriented around words or messages. So Twitter just didn't fit, and we were fine with that.

At this point our annual revenue had grown to six figures. Facebook was a significant source of referral traffic, as we'd learned to use the fan page system to attract and engage with new prospects. And we learned to cost effectively use the advertising systems in both YouTube and Facebook. So our success on those platforms was via both organic and paid growth.

A Funny Thing Happened

As we checked our website analytics, we saw a new social network popping up—Pinterest. In the summer of 2011, Pinterest was like any other website to us, a blip on our website stats page. It was referring traffic, but not enough to even make us curious. We certainly didn't have the time or energy to invest in another social media website, and so we ignored it. However, by October 2011 we were increasingly excited about what Pinterest was doing for us. It became our hot topic.

We now had three social media traffic sources of significance: Facebook, YouTube, and Pinterest. Pinterest was gaining ground so quickly, we could see it would soon become our top source. The crazy part was, we hadn't even set up a Pinterest profile yet. This referral traffic was being generated by our customers and fans as they shared our products with their friends.

By late November 2011, we decided it was time to take Pinterest seriously. We wondered what would happen to our traffic stats once we were able to actually start working on Pinterest to drive even more traffic. By early December, we set up our account. We also decided to publicly blog about our experiences and setup (http://www.marketing onpinterest.com). We documented our Four-Step Marketing Plan and began sharing our lessons learned.

As we thought might happen, our referral traffic from Pinterest zoomed up. The month after we started on Pinterest, it had doubled. By January 2012, Pinterest had become our top social media referral source, way ahead of both Facebook and YouTube. The realization that all our work and effort for several years on Facebook and YouTube was being eclipsed by Pinterest so quickly was both thrilling and depressing. It was, and continues to be, almost too good to be true.

By March 2012 we had passed over 1,000 followers on our primary Pinterest account (see Figure 4.1). As of this writing we continue to refine and enhance activities to boost our traffic from Pinterest.

Figure 4.1 Cinnamon Miles and the Liberty Jane Clothing profile after four months on Pinterest.

Lessons We Learned

As time has gone by, we've analyzed our experiences carefully, and here is the essence of what we learned:

- E-mail marketing is the original and best form of online marketing. Google can "slap" you, your Facebook page can be shut down, and your YouTube videos can be removed. Even your Pinterest account could be suspended. However, your e-mail list is a stable and important business asset that you control in a unique and powerful way. Learn to drive all social media traffic into your e-mail capture system. (See Chapter 16.)

- Success in e-mail marketing leads to success in social networks as you simply share what you're doing on a new social network. Convert your current e-mail subscribers into followers on the new social site. Boom, instant followers!

- Success on one social network leads to success on a second social network, and this leads to success on future social network sites. This happens for a couple of reasons. First, you learn how to quickly operate in those environments without a lot of drama. Second, you can invite all your followers from one site into the next and expand your influence.

- Don't feel the need to participate in every social network. If one isn't right for you, then forget it, as we did with Twitter.

- Social networks provide the most important kind of traffic—endorsed traffic. Of all the social networks we've encountered, Pinterest is the absolute best for endorsed traffic. So if there is one social network you ought to consider participating in, Pinterest is it.

- Pinterest saves you a huge amount of time because so much of the pinning is done by other people.

- You're getting in on the early days of Pinterest, as its forecasted growth rates are astounding. By getting in early, you have a chance to ride the wave as more and more people catch on to the power of Pinterest.

Part 2

PINTEREST
FOR
MARKETERS

Basic Functions and Beginner Best Bets

Within the world of Pinterest lie alleyways of interest and benefit to you. Over time you will discover these on your own; however, why not take the fast track? Whether you're a complete newbie to the Pinterest experience, a person who's signed up and ready but hasn't really caught onto the magic, or a seasoned veteran already reaping the benefits, this chapter will hold a nugget or 10 for you.

Navigating the website and setting up your Pinterest foundation correctly will build you a secure, earthquakeproof experience down the road. Pinterest can be used for pure play and inspiration, and in fact, we recommend you incorporate this into your plan. Inspiration leads to new ideas and avenues, each created by a spark of passion. But concrete techniques can be applied to get you better results faster. Quickly and easily maneuvering to where you need to go, along with learning how to present yourself when you get there, will set you up early for success. After all, reinventing the wheel is overrated at best, hard work at worst.

Some Terminology

Pinterest isn't just changing the way people discover new things on the web; it's also changing the basic layout of many Internet sites and the terminology that surrounds them. In this book, we'll be using traditional terminology, as well as updated lingo. Let's look at the basic terms:

- **Web page.** Easy. We all know that when we go online, we look at *pages*. You'll find us discussing the Profile page, Pinners You Follow page, and so on.

- **Grid design or grid layout.** This is where Pinterest is changing the basic setup of a page. The classic Pinterest page is formatted in a grid design or layout. Images are arranged horizontally and vertically, in a somewhat linear fashion as they fit. This is the grid. So it's technically correct to think of your Profile page as your Profile grid. (As an aside, watch how many websites start using the grid layout. You'll be amazed.)

- **Feed or browsing feed.** This is the stream of images that's filling the grids within your pages. Each grid has a feed.

That's it for now. Let's get started.

The Basics

Let's begin at the top. The upper Pinterest toolbar is full of information, cool tools, and search possibilities. It's not completely intuitive, and so we'll walk you through the features.

The central, red Pinterest button takes you straight to your Pinners You Follow page (also called grid) where recent pinning activity is displayed. You'll see your own pins, as well as those of the people you follow. On the left side of the page under Recent Activity, you'll be updated on the latest 15 pins, likes, and comments on your images. The Pinners You Follow page displays the Pinterest community you're developing. The big red button will get you back here every time.

Beneath the central Pinterest button are several choices. The Pinners You Follow page is, as described above, where your pins and those of the people you follow are displayed.

Hovering your mouse over Everything will show a drop-down menu where you can navigate to the 32 Pinterest content categories. Categories are important, and your images need to be correctly labeled to get the maximum benefit when people search. As well, this is a place where you can go to find great images. You can generate new ideas, inspiration, and oodles of content for your own projects.

Next, click on Videos. Pinterest isn't that well known for sharing videos, but it has a great setup for doing so, and this area might grow rapidly. You'll find everything from home videos, to popular songs, to how-tos, to inspirational tales.

The Popular grid (also called page) is one of the most important areas for your small-business plan. From here you can identify key influencers to follow and dramatically expand your reach. Because the culture of Pinterest is to find and display exceptional images, you will want to get your original content (images from your website) onto the Popular grid and benefit from the phenomenal stream of repins.

For example, if your original content gets pinned a few times, you may see a few clicks back to your website every month. However, if you get lucky enough to have a piece land on the Popular grid, it may get pinned hundreds or even thousands of times. In this way, it goes viral and creates an enormous flow of traffic back to your site. The goal is to create content that both represents your business well and also has a universal message that appeals to everyone.

So the next logical question for every smart marketer is, how do you create content that has the potential to go viral? Or at the very least, how do you create images that get onto the Popular grid? There's no hard-and-fast solution, but if you follow our best practices in the next two chapters, the odds will be boosted in your favor.

In Figure 5.1, this one image by Liz Marie Galvan was pinned from her blog over 22,000 times. Now that's going viral. The amount of repins from those 22,000 will be many times more. It's called smart marketing on Pinterest.

Finally, Gifts refers to products for sale with price banners. Viewers click on the image to go to the corresponding website. Hovering your mouse over Gifts will provide a drop-down menu with different price ranges. This feature is powerful because people come here actively searching for things to buy. As you expand your Pinterest marketing, you'll want to take full advantage of this area.

Adding a price banner to your image is easy. In the description box when you are pinning or repinning an image, type in the price with a dollar sign within your description. The system then automatically turns this into a price banner in the upper left-hand corner of the image.

⇅ Repin   Edit   From lizmarieblog.com

Makeup brush organization. Makeup brush love :)
Pinned via pinmarklet

Figure 5.1 An example from lizmarie.blog of an image that went viral with over 22,000 pins.

The remaining features on the top toolbar include a keyword search box on the left. Pretty straightforward. On the right side of the toolbar, if you click on Add+, you can add a pin manually (that is, without using the Pin It button) and create new pinboards. Hover your mouse over either About or your name—both will bring up drop-down menus with a selection of options. From here you invite friends, manage your profile and account, and learn more about Pinterest. The big red Invite Friends button walks you through the options for doing just that.

The Power of a Profile

A key component of your success with Pinterest is finding that fine balance between presenting yourself as professional and yet being friendly and approachable. Those that do this well more easily attract followers and repins. Other than your actual pins, your Profile page is where viewers will first begin to learn about you. They'll see your picture or logo and begin to form an impression—a first impression. And we all know how important that is. Take some time to think about how you want your viewers to first see you.

Access your Profile page by clicking on your name and picture in the top right-hand corner. At the top of the page sits a brief profile of you. Here you can upload a picture or logo and write a tagline about yourself and the message you want to share with viewers. For the small-business owner, this message should be fun and light, but it should also clearly reveal the style of what you do. Beneath your profile, all your pinboards are laid out in a grid.

In Figure 5.2, you can see that ModCloth uses a professional yet friendly approach for its profile. The tagline is fun and appeals to the very core attractions that Pinterest has tapped into: visual enticement, creativity, and a passion for things that we love and are inspired by. A professional logo is used, and the overall brand is appealing. With almost 17,000 followers, ModCloth must be doing something right!

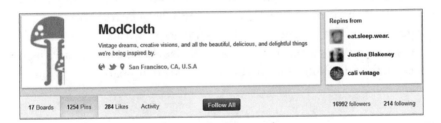

Figure 5.2 ModCloth has a great profile that achieves a professional yet friendly style.

TRAFFIC TIPS

When you create your profile, use either a professional head shot or a logo. Start immediately with the message that you're professional. Next, create a tagline of one or two sentences that both intrigues the viewer and gets across what you do. Check out what other people are saying about themselves to get a feel for what might work for you.

Your Profile page is full of information. It's where viewers can see all your boards and get a real feel for who you are and what matters to you. When you view other peoples' Profile pages, you also get to know them and see which people you have something in common with and want to follow. Check out their profiles by clicking on their user name whenever you see it. This will occur if you see their pin or if they comment, like, or repin your images.

Navigating a Profile page is easy. Beneath the profile sits a toolbar listing how many boards you've created and how many total pins you've made, including both original pins and repins. It also tells you how many times your pins have been liked, and the Activity button will show you all your recent Pinterest activity.

Click on Edit Profile to change your picture, tagline, e-mail address, and password. You can also do this by hovering your mouse over your name and picture in the upper right-hand corner and clicking on Settings.

On your own Profile page (but not someone else's), you can also rearrange the order of your pinboards, as in Figure 5.3. This is a great tool to make sure the most visually enticing or helpful boards are at the beginning and thus are seen first. This strategy goes back to the first impression you want to make. Hover your mouse over the little square icon next to the Edit Profile button. Click on Rearrange boards.

Figure 5.3 Fine-tuning your Profile page by arranging the order of your pinboards will help you create a great first impression for viewers.

To further tailor your Profile page, you can even choose which pin will appear first on each board and thereby fill up the larger top image. Click on the pinboard to bring up all its images; then hover your mouse over the pin you want to be the first up. Click on Set Board Cover.

TRAFFIC TIP

To make sure your boards fit perfectly within the board cover space allotted, use images that are proportionate rectangles of 4 × 6. An image of 400 pixels tall by 600 pixels wide will appear completely in the board cover, rather than being cut off.

Basic Pinboard and Pin Functions

To view a specific board, simply click on it. Up will come every image pinned, along with statistics on how many times it's been repinned and liked and the string of comments, if any. This is a great source of information because you can quickly see which boards became most popular. Learn from this; it will serve you well.

If you're viewing someone's board and it inspires you, click on the red Follow button to begin following the person's new pins. When you're on the person's Profile page, where all his or her boards are displayed (get there by clicking on the person's name), you can choose Follow All if you want to follow all the boards. Or you can select individual boards only.

Next let's look at the nuances of a single pin. Click on any image on a board or on a page, and up will come that specific image. Included will be details about who pinned it and from where, as well as all the repins, likes, and comments. To make a comment on the pin, just write what you want to say in the comment box and click Post Comment.

By clicking on the pinned image, you will be taken directly to the source from which it was originally pinned. Ideally this is to the original website or blog where you can either learn more about the idea or product or purchase it outright.

Keep scrolling down the pin, and a plethora of information will appear, as in Figure 5.4. Here you can see who pinned the image and from what board. You also learn who pinned the image originally and from what source. Then the entire string of repins is listed. This information will come in handy as you begin to repin and follow those that repin your images. We'll discuss this concept more in Chapter 7.

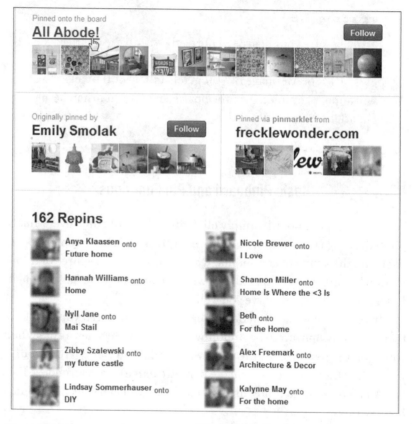

Figure 5.4 At the bottom of a pin lies a wealth of information about the history of that specific image on Pinterest.

Pinning Photos from Your Computer

The advantages of pinning content from your own website or blog will be discussed at length in the next chapter. Part of this process might entail pinning your personal photographs from your computer files. Fortunately, this is easy to do.

1. Click on Add+ in the top right-hand corner of any page.

2. Click on Upload a Pin.

3. Browse your files and click on the photo or image you want to add.

4. Choose a category and describe the pin. Then click on Pin It.

5. The most critical part occurs once you pin your image. You must go back and link it to your website or blog. When you upload a picture from your computer, it has nowhere to link back to. So click on your newly pinned image. Then click on Edit. Paste your website URL here. Be sure you paste the URL of the exact page you want people to visit.

    If you're not familiar with how to paste a URL, it's easy. Bring up the relevant page on your Internet browser. Highlight the address that appears in the upper toolbar—this is the URL. Copy this address and then paste where appropriate.

Advanced Pinboarding

When you first begin working with Pinterest, you will find pinboards readymade for you. This is fine for getting started, but not good enough for our purposes. The power of the pinboard is immense and often lies at the heart of how much traction you're getting.

Let's look at ways you can up the ante and make your pinboards irresistible to follow and repin from.

Narrow Your Focus

The first thing to keep in mind is that pinboards with titles such as "Stuff I Love" and "Cool Things" are great to share with family and friends and to give a feel for you as a person. But for marketing purposes, those titles are way too broad. Unless we know you personally, and maybe not even then, we won't have a clue what "cool stuff" might be in your eyes. This makes it difficult to get excited about the images and ideas you might have to share. These types of boards can be used as an addition to your overall presentation, but not as the main focus.

On the other hand, if you narrow the focus of your pinboards, people will be able to see exactly what you have to offer and can more easily decide to become involved. The key is to arrange each board around a theme. ModCloth's "Vintage Vantage" board immediately tells anyone interested in vintage clothing and style to go here (Figure 2.1). How about Sha Hwang's "Gifts for the Nerdy Designer." You have an immediate sense of what to expect from these boards. And most important, they're intriguing. Play around with titles until you find just the right combination of information and fun.

With Facebook and Twitter, fans have to follow all the posted content whether they're interested or not, but with Pinterest you only have to follow those pinboards that specifically appeal to you. As a marketer, you can turn this into a distinct advantage. Form a theme for each board, the narrower the better, and then group themed boards together. If recipes are your thing, you can have "Cool Summer Soups," "Autumn Harvest Bake-Off," and "Homemade Halloween Treats."

Get creative. Have fun!

Multiple Pinners

Sometimes you might want to set up a pinboard so that more than one person can add pins. This is useful if you want to get your followers more directly involved in your boards (and for planning events like the family summer reunion). It's one more marketing opportunity at your fingertips.

You can add more pinners when you create the board, or you can do it later by clicking on the Edit Board button on the toolbar at the top of each board. Under Who Can Pin? click on Me + Contributors. Then invite each person you want to allow access to. The person must accept the invitation to complete the process.

Categories

Categories are important, and you'll see us refer to them several times throughout the book. For this chapter, what's crucial is that you make sure each image you pin is properly categorized. If a viewer searches for images via that specific category, "Home Decor" for example, and your unique and eye-appealing lamp shades aren't categorized properly, the viewer won't see your images. An opportunity lost.

One problem arises when you see a must-pin image on a website and go to pin it but you don't have a board that suits the category.

Pinterest allows you to create a board during the process of pinning. However, this is the catch: that board won't belong to a category unless you go in manually *afterward* to the Edit Board feature and attach it to one. If you find the perfect picture of those 4-inch tiger-striped high heels, go ahead and create a new pinboard as you pin the image. But you must later categorize it manually if you want it to be searchable under "Women's Apparel."

Pinboard Taglines

Using taglines for each pinboard is a great way to further communicate your message. For example, Sha Hwang has a board entitled "Field Aesthetics." From the initial images, you can see right away that this is full of appealing and unique designs. However, when you click on the board, you're able to read his short tagline that explains the board's purpose in more detail: "Beautiful things in hoards."

This is your opportunity to tell your viewer a bit more about your vision and passion. It's another area in which you can express yourself and create a stronger link.

To create a tagline, click on the board and then on Edit Board. In the Description box, fill in your tagline, as in Figure 5.5. When you're done, click Save Settings.

Keywords

They're not gone yet. Keywords are still a common way for people to search within Pinterest too. Therefore, you must make yourself available to this feature. When a viewer types in what he or she is looking for in the keyword search box, you need to be set up to properly position yourself in the results. The following are ways to do this:

- When you name your board, include a keyword that people might search by. Instead of "Summer Clothes," how about "Tank Tops," "Sundresses," and "Summer Sandals."

- When you type in a description of your pin, choose specific words that could show up in a search. You don't have to change your style; just tweak the words a bit. If you pinned or repinned an image of a line of dinner candles, don't just say "Wow, aren't they beautiful?!" How about "Wow, aren't these dinner votives beautiful?!"

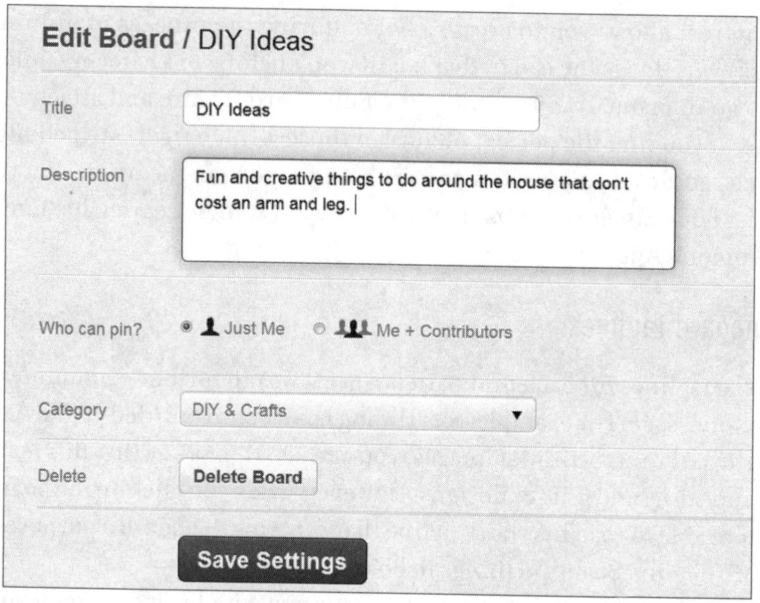

Edit Board / DIY Ideas

Title
> DIY Ideas

Description
> Fun and creative things to do around the house that don't cost an arm and leg. |

Who can pin?   ● 👤 Just Me   ○ 👥 Me + Contributors

Category
> DIY & Crafts ▼

Delete
> **Delete Board**

Save Settings

Figure 5.5 The pinboard tagline allows you to more clearly express your ideas and passion.

In Summary

The Pinterest experience can certainly be profitable, but it should also be fun and inspiring. Life is much more enjoyable this way. Follow these rules for setting yourself up right:

- Pin and repin what you love.

- Use great images—humorous, helpful, inspiring, or just plain beautiful; these all work wonders.

- Organize your boards, profile, and taglines to get across your message in a fun and intriguing way.

- Don't just find inspiration; give it back too.

- Be social. Repin, like, and comment on what other people care about.

- Follow people whose images inspire you.

Pinning for Maximum Success

*A*s you experience more of what Pinterest has to offer, you will realize that some users consistently pin images that speak to your mind and soul, while others leave you with a big question mark hanging over your head. You're left wondering what they were thinking pinning that picture of granny's old blue rocker. But take a step back. What's important to one person might be unfathomable to another, and that's the nature of self-expression. We don't all like the same food, music, movies, or fashion, because we're each and every one of us a unique individual.

For the small-business owner, this is an advantage. Not every person is your ideal client. Not everyone will value your message and product or service. Through Pinterest, you are able to develop your niche by expressing who you are, which in turn creates a highly qualified pool of potential clients. Specific pinning techniques will help you do this for maximum effectiveness. As you refine your style and become more proficient at finding and creating great content, you will develop a following on Pinterest of people who respond to you and your vision. These people will then help you grow your business.

We asked the team at Pinterest this question:

Q. There is an enormous range of marketing behaviors that could occur on Pinterest, some evil, like spam; some less evil, like contests; and some very simple, like branding strategies. Is there an ideal "use case" that marketers can adopt that you'd affirm? Is there any specific tactic, besides the obvious spam issues, that you'd say is less desirable?

A. For brands, pinning can be a great way to highlight aspects of your brand that may not come to mind at first when people consider your brand or company. As we state in our brand guidelines, as simple as it sounds, best practices for using Pinterest for brand purposes center around pinning like a regular user.

Most important, this includes:

- Pinning from various sources rather than one specific site.

- Repinning from within the site to engage with others—repinning is one of the most social activities on Pinterest, and it's how any user really builds a network of followers.

- Creating at least a few boards that cover a broad range of interests, rather than maintaining a single board devoted to one topic.

Let's look at how you can achieve this.

You Are What You Pin

What you pin lies at the very core of Pinterest. To begin with, it's what draws us to this website in the first place. We get to see great images and share our own. Second, the images and videos we pin are how we express ourselves, which means they're how other people learn about us. When you take the time to cruise through people's pinboards, you learn what makes them laugh, what makes them smile, what their values are, and what they find most important in this world—all through a few virtual pinboards. As Ben Silbermann comments:

> What you learn about a person through their collections is very true to who they are.

It's as if through these pinned images, we have finally found a venue to celebrate our lives and the world around us. At the most basic level, we are wired to be social and to express ourselves. Along with this is a core drive to contribute to the world and our community—and then, in return, to be acknowledged for this contribution. It's literally in our DNA. And it's in the virtual DNA of Pinterest to facilitate this need.

TRAFFIC TIP

Just as it's an integral part of Pinterest to express yourself through images and videos, it's an equally core part to acknowledge the images and videos of others. We seek recognition, as does everyone else. To become an active member of this community and help create a great following, be sure and give more then you receive. Repin, like, and comment on what speaks to you. People will feel appreciated and return the favor.

As you stay true to your message and consistently pin high-quality images (for finding out how to do this, stay tuned), you will become known for this content. Genuine bonds are formed as people connect through their tastes. These people will become your advocates and help your small business grow, as you will theirs.

We'll show you how to aggregate great content and even how to build your own. The key lies in delivering value—at Pinterest this means being unique, helpful, and visually startling. You can accumulate content that will appear at the same level as that of any professional site. And this will be what expresses who you are. How cool is that?

But how will you know if you're tapping into that primordial nerve that will garner a massive, quality following? The tools are right in front of you. In order to improve on something, we must first be able to measure it. To measure it, we must first be able to track it. At Pinterest this is done through the number of repins, likes, and comments you receive, with repins being the most valuable because these carry the link back to your website or blog.

Eight Keys to Becoming a Trusted Resource

Fortunately, you don't have to create all this wonderful content you're going to be known by. You're going to become content curators. What's that you ask, something from a museum? Well, sort of. You've probably already been a content curator in your life without necessarily knowing it. Have you ever burned your own music CD or created an iPod collection of all your favorite songs? Were you involved in making the family cookbook with recipes spanning from ones from your 10-year-old daughter to ones from great-great-grandma Rita Mae?

Both these are examples of curating content. All it really means is gathering great stuff from the entire universe and putting it together in one collection. Voilà! You're a curator.

The funny thing is, at Pinterest you begin by curating images and end by curating *people.* You will collect followers who understand and love your vision and want to experience more. In other words, you will collect people who appreciate you. But you must be faithful to them, or you'll quickly fall into the realm of the "unfollowed."

Below are eight keys to help you pin content that's personal, professional, and passionate. These keys will help create a real expression of your brand that will filter through to expanding your business.

1. **Pin your passion.** This is the most crucial key and one you've heard us mention before. Pin images and videos that mean something to you and resonate with who you are. If it doesn't make your heart speed up a tick or two, don't pin it. Full stop.

> **In Jason's words:** Not long ago I started following a social media expert. He was someone who was supposed to be a real go-to guy, and I wanted to learn from him. Little did I realize, he commonly pinned lewd images and crude humor. I could only tolerate it for a day or so until I realized that I just don't see the world the way he does, and I certainly didn't want to follow him anymore. Maybe if he'd stopped to consider what he was doing, he'd have realized he was alienating potential customers. As Shakespeare said, "Mend your speech a little, lest you may mar your fortunes."

2. **The devil's in the details.** We like people with whom we share things in common. It makes us feel good when someone else has the same taste we do. For a marketer, this means sharing things that are specific that potential customers can bond to. If it's too vague, you won't attract the qualified traffic you're seeking. Football, fashion, and religion are fine. But how about Colts fans, eye makeup aficionados, and Baptists. The narrower your target, the higher quality your referral traffic.

3. **Impress, inspire, startle.** While you've heard it before from us, it's worth reemphasizing here. Pin the best images you can find. The pins that go viral are visually startling, unique, funny, or helpful. Search for the best images and videos possible within your niches. Leave ho-hum at the door.

4. **Let yourself shine.** We each have a unique personality just waiting to be expressed, and here's where you can share it to once again amplify the bonding experience. The better people feel they know you, the more comfortable they'll be in trusting your recommendations, including buying your products or services. Do you have a funky or sarcastic sense of humor? Show it! Do you like funny sayings? Pin them. Everyone loves the good chuckle that comes from seeing the world from a humorous angle. Let your personality out, and it will attract people who appreciate you. (See Figure 6.1.)

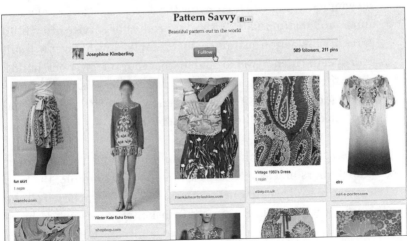

Figure 6.1 Josephine Kimberling lets her artistic personality shine in her "Pattern Savvy" pinboard.

5. **Integrity.** While some of us are a little more gullible than others, eventually we all can smell dishonesty and falseness a cybermile away. Over time it oozes through every pore of the dishonest person's essence. People need to know that they can trust you and that you will always lead them in a good and healthy direction. The best way to achieve this? Just do it. Always keep the best interest of others in mind, and they will quickly sense that you are the type of person they want to be associated with. Maintaining a high level of integrity will pay off big over the medium and long term.

6. **Social proof.** There's no getting around it—life is like high school. People like to be around popular people. Look how as a culture we worship movie stars and musicians. We might not even know what they're like as individuals, but we sure would like to be up close and personal. This is part of why it's so important to get as many followers as possible on Pinterest. Popularity feeds upon itself. After all, if you're so popular, you must have some good stuff to share.

7. **Guarantees and testimonials.** As Pinterest grows, the number of scammers, con artists, and overall less-than-desirables will grow too. There's no doubt that Pinterest will do everything in its power to filter these bottom feeders out, but some will slip through. To set yourself apart, consider using the dual-edged sword of guarantees and testimonials. With your product or service offer a 100 percent satisfaction guarantee, for example—or whatever will suit your specific niche. And to double-coat your integrity net, build a pinboard of client testimonials, or at the very least have a testimonial page on your website. Let users know you're the real thing and a safe place to harbor their e-commerce boat.

8. **Get personal.** As you share images of things you love, remember to share personal aspects of your life too. For example, the hottest star in Hollywood won't get the same type of traction if all she does is post images taken directly from her movie scenes. If, however, she pins images of her home and family and dog, the viewers will instantly feel a much higher degree of connection and therefore attraction. The same thing will work for you, albeit at a non-

Hollywood-star level. Let people get to know you personally. Create pinboards that show the hang-out-in-shorts-and-T-shirt you, not just the outer layer of products and ideas.

The Three Ps of Becoming a Trusted Resource

If you follow the above eight keys, you will see an increase in the quality and quantity of referral traffic to your website or blog. Let's tie it all together using the three Ps of principle, practice, and profit.

Principle. Becoming a trusted provider is crucial to developing a high-quality, loyal following. You will become known as an excellent resource for information and inspiration.

Practice. Achieving this status isn't just a matter of finding cool images; it also entails applying every one of the eight keys outlined above. You want to be known as a real person who has the users' interests in mind and will always do the best for them. Plus you pin really cool images.

Profit. The principle and practice of becoming a trusted resource will lead not only to more referral traffic but to referral traffic of higher quality. Because you've narrowed down your targeted clients to those who specifically like your products and like you, you will achieve a higher conversion rate from prospects to sales.

Curating and Creating Killer Content

Herein lies one of the core nubs of success: how to find and create content that people will follow. You will most likely begin your Pinterest experience by pinning other people's images. But the end goal is to get the viewer back to your website or blog, and to do this you need to pin images from these locations.

Interestingly, the first step to take in your search for content is to get a clear picture of who your ideal clients are. Begin with the end, so to speak. If you know who would most like your products or services, you'll know how to appeal to them visually.

In this next section, we'll cover three aspects of curating and creating killer content:

1. The client

2. Where to find the good stuff

3. Creating your own content

The Client

To develop a focused idea of your ideal clients, take into account the following 10 questions. By carefully answering each one, you will be well on your way to understanding your clients like never before. Through understanding, lies opportunity.

1. Why would people be interested in your niche? Make a list of as many reasons as you can think of.

2. Do they have fears and frustrations that could be addressed?

3. What do they enjoy most about this niche?

4. What different end goals will they achieve with your product or service?

5. What are they most passionate about in relation to these end goals?

6. How can you help them achieve these passions and goals?

7. Will there be other hobbies or interests these people might share?

8. Are they generally affluent or thrifty?

9. Are they conservative or progressive?

10. Do they share a faith, belief system, or worldview that resonates with you?

Write out your answers to each of these questions and carefully consider the information you've come up with. By understanding what's most important to your potential clients, you can most effectively fill their needs. And filling their needs is what it's all about.

Armed with this new knowledge, you can create pinboards that will address the hottest topics. These people will know that you understand their interests and fears and can address them.

Where to Find the Good Stuff

Now that you know your ideal client more intimately, it will be that much easier to find great content because the first step is taken care of—what the heck it is you're looking for! By knowing the end result, you know what's best to pin.

So now where do we go? Well, it may seem obvious, but finding images on Pinterest and repinning them is an excellent place to start. Not only is it a site dedicated to displaying great images; it's also a way to develop relationships. As you repin, like, and comment, folks will notice you and do the same back. To narrow your searches, use the Everything feature and search by category, and also use the keyword search box in the upper left-hand corner.

Out in the wild and woolly world of the Internet, find blogs and websites that are dedicated to the same niches and interests you are. If rainbow lorikeets are your thing, search with Google or another search engine by the specific name, but also related keywords, such as *parrot experts, Australian parrots, best parrot care,* and the like. You can be stuck here for hours, but it'll be worth your time. Don't forget to use the Images button on the Google left-side menu. You don't want to pin directly from these images because they won't carry the original website link to Pinterest with them. But you can see what images are available, click on them, and be taken to the corresponding website.

Tap within your own network. If you're looking to expand your designer cupcake business, what other people do you know who bake these marvelous creations? Do they have resources they go to for ideas and inspiration? Are they willing to talk with you about what you're doing with Pinterest and provide advice? Within all these avenues you will find sources of great content for pinning.

Sometimes niche-specific content is found on sites without any pinnable images. For example, Wikipedia has loads of information, but you can't pin it. TED videos are insanely popular but, again, not easily pinnable. Fortunately, there's an easy fix. Create an image of your own, pin it, and then link it to the content you want to share that isn't pinnable. The easiest way to do this is to Photoshop a new image.

To link the new pin to a specific site, pin the image and then click Edit. Here you can paste a link to wherever you want the viewer to go.

Here is a specific example from Jason's pinboards, in Jason's words: Wikipedia has a terrific entry on pricing models, where it outlines 22 proven models. But there is no pinnable image associated with the entry, which is true of almost all the Wikipedia content. So in order to add this information to my pricing board, "Pricing Nerd, Yes I Am," I created a simple graphic that said "22 Pricing Models that are proven to work." I pinned that image and pasted the URL for the Wikipedia article. The 600 people who follow my "Pricing" pinboard will be grateful that I've done this work and am sharing this valuable information.

TRAFFIC TIP

Some websites have blocked the Pinterest bookmarklet tool because of copyright concerns. Never circumvent this by creating your own image and pointing it to those sites. Honor the original content owners' wishes.

Creating Your Own Content

This is where the pedal hits the metal. You must eventually pin content from your own website or blog. This will carry the links that will come back in the form of potential business. If you have images available already, great. Pin these following the guidelines of focused boards. However, as you progress, you will continually need to add more of your own content. One way to do this is to create your own.

Two issues exist regarding the creation of your own content to pin. The first is how to create the image and general ideas for the type of format you intend to use, e.g., photographs versus videos. The second relates to the actual content within the pin. What's your message and call

TRAFFIC TIP

Be sure to trickle your own images in over time rather than pin them all at once. If you just dump them in, their effect will be diluted. If, however, you add them gradually, you see which ones work the best and keep your followers waiting for more.

to action for the prospective clients? Below we handle the first aspect, how to create your pins. For creating the most effective content within the pins, see Chapter 10, the section titled "Pins with Punch." Also read the blogger success stories in Chapter 11. These will both arm you with an excellent array of content options to choose from.

If you're handy with photography and Photoshop-type software, creating your own pins is a natural. You know how to take pictures and make them even better with digital tools. Graphics can be added for an even more professional touch. Eventually you will be creating videos, infographics, tutorials, and more.

If you don't have these skills, you have some options. One, learn how. Myriad online courses exist for just these purposes. Maybe a local college or community center will have classes if a more personal touch is your preference. Two, hire someone to do it for you. While this might not be the cheapest alternative in the short term, it will most probably produce the professional results you're seeking. Consider doing this for a few key niche ideas at the beginning until you see that the effort is paying off.

Finally, consider tapping your social network and finding a graphic artist or designer you could work with for mutual benefit. The artist could create your images, and you could promote the artist on your site, for example.

Blogging is a simple tool to go hand in hand with creating your own content. Post your picture, infographic, or any combination on your blog to accompany an article you've written. This way, Pinterest folks will be directed not only to your blog but also to your expertise. We all like a picture to visualize what we're reading. Use this to make your blog more interesting—and to have original content for your pinboards.

The Three Ps of Killer Content

It's not rocket science to understand that on a site as visual as Pinterest, the better your content, the more followers you'll attract. Let's look at how the three Ps lead us straight to more profits.

Principle. Killer content combined with a solid reputation for being a trusted resource will get you more quality followers on Pinterest. By pinning content from your own website or blog, you create the links that will direct people to your products and services.

Practice. Three phases will get you nose to nose with this content:

- First, know your ideal clients inside and out. Answer the questions in "The Client" section earlier in the chapter and any others you think will help you get closer to who they are and what they value most.

- Second, search Pinterest, other search engines like Google, and your own network of niche experts to find resources of valuable images and ideas. Remember, it often happens that one resource leads to another, which leads to another, and on and on.

- Third, create your own images by using Photoshop or by hiring or collaborating with an expert, and post these to accompany articles on your blog or website. Then pin these images onto your pinboards, and interested users will be taken straight back to the source—you.

Profit. Knowing who your clients are allows you to pin content that will speak directly to their hearts and souls, not to mention whatever hobby or skill they're pursuing. When you then follow this up with pinning the very best, specific images, you will gain more qualified followers. Add to the mix poignant images from your own website or blog. The more qualified followers you have, the more business you will generate.

Know your clients and speak to them. Herein lies the power of Pinterest.

Copyright Issues

You may have heard stories about copyright issues in relation to pinning photographs and art that isn't yours. Concerns have been voiced that if you post someone else's photo of his delicious roast beef recipe, or pin an image from someone's blog of her children playing with a Labrador retriever, you may be violating copyright laws. Scary thoughts and something we all need to be aware of.

We're not lawyers and can't give you legal advice. However, what we can supply is a good dose of common sense. If and when copyright issues become a problem, you can count on it that we'll all hear about them. Pinterest itself will be the first to announce any changes and requirements that we need to follow. After all, it's in Pinterest's best interests to keep us pinning as much as possible because that's the entire purpose of Pinterest—to share fabulous images of the things we love. So for now, it would appear we can happily pin away to our hearts' content.

We asked Pinterest directly about copyright issues:

Q. We write about best practices for copyright issues in the book. Is there any additional advice you'd give for marketers, especially small businesses, related to this issue?

A. The best advice can be found in our Pin Etiquette around crediting your sources:

> Credit Your Sources: Pins are the most useful when they have links back to the original source. If you notice that a pin is not sourced correctly, leave a comment so the original pinner can update the source. Finding the original source is always preferable to a secondary source such as Image Search or a blog entry.

But as Pinterest suggests, you can take prudent and community-spirited steps to make sure credit is given where credit is due. When you post a photo, make sure the source is fully credited, especially if it's someone's photograph or graphic art. This may not always be possible because links get lost. But if you're pinning images from other sources, you can do your part to keep the community clean. Always credit your sources. Always make sure they link to the original source.

Think of how you would want your original pins to be credited to you, and do that for other people. Follow the Golden Rule.

Part 3

LEVERAGING THE POWER OF PINTEREST

Strategies for Social Contagion

*M*ost likely, to one degree or another, you already have a presence on another social media site. You might heavily utilize this
site to generate as much business as possible. Or you could be
one of the many that check their Facebook accounts religiously every . . .
week, and mainly then to catch up on funny pictures and videos. These
sites serve all these purposes: from engaging in casual social interaction to spearheading marketing within a thriving business; each set of
needs can be filled.

In this respect, Pinterest is no different. The site can be used as an
easygoing place to store holiday craft ideas, just as it can truly alter the
profit-and-loss landscape of your small business. If you're searching
for the latter, Pinterest has a set of features that when used properly will
foster a virtual social contagion of your images and ideas. By maximiz-
ing the tools and quirks of the Pinterest experience, you can become a
rainmaker within this new community.

First you must understand the strengths and weaknesses of the
tools you have to work with and therefore how to optimize your efforts.
Similarities exist among the various social media sites, and so do differences. Learning how to integrate your business within these social
communities will open the opportunity to dramatically increase sales.

Who Are You?

Let's go back to thinking about how you want to first position yourself on Pinterest. You know about the need to present yourself in a personal yet professional way, and you are clued in on pinning great content. But yet another choice exists: Are you a business where one key individual is the main figurehead and spokesperson? Or would you rather have the company brand and logo be the virtual storefront? Both options work no matter the size of your business.

Josephine Kimberling, a successful surface designer and licensing artist, presents herself as an individual on Pinterest. She's a great example of the personality profile approach, and first thing on her Profile page she directs viewers to her website, http://www.josephinekimberling.com.

Kimberling notes:

> Using Pinterest has been a great asset for my life and business because it has allowed me to capture in one place many things that inspire me, in an organized way, so I have a quick point of reference when researching. It also allows me to connect with other creatives out in the world; to inspire and be inspired by each other.

ModCloth, whose Profile page we looked at in Chapter 5, generates phenomenal business through Pinterest using the company brand. ModCloth made the choice of putting its brand at the forefront of Pinterest rather than any one individual.

Both paths work; your only job is to choose which will suit your situation the best. Let's look at some pros and cons of each.

The Personality Profile

The personality profile functions well within the full spectrum of business: from sole proprietors to big names like Martha Stewart, Oprah, and Rachael Ray. In each case you associate the business with a specific individual and style.

The upside of a person representing the Pinterest profile is that potential customers can quickly bond with you as an individual. They see you as an expert and go-to resource for ideas and inspiration, but also as a real person they can relate to. Don't underestimate the power here. If you're a one-stop shop or a start-up, consider this alternative. You can always change to a company brand down the road.

The potential pitfall within using yourself as the spokesperson for your business is the risk of losing privacy. As you become well known and attract more followers, you may not enjoy the conflicting cross-winds of your professional social media life interfering with your private one. Your Pinterest profile, Facebook page, blog, etc., will potentially be bombarded with business-related followers and comments. Some people love the limelight; others run for shade. It's a truly personal decision.

The Corporate Profile

One upside of using the company brand as the face of your business is that social media sites can be managed by anyone. If you have staffing changes, or just want to take a well-deserved vacation, someone else can seamlessly handle the day-to-day maintenance. Another aspect is that if this is a business with more than one founder or key employee, who would be the representative? If you use the company brand, this doesn't become an issue. As well, maybe it's just not your style to have a single personality represent the company. This is certainly a valid issue.

A downside is that you run the risk of losing that personal connection, because there is no "person" that the client can see and relate to. You can overcome this by creating an appealing, personal brand and a consistent and engaging pinning method that bonds with your viewers. It's all possible; you just need to put extra thought here.

The Social Cycle

Have you ever wondered why social media is so popular? If you're over the age of 30, you most probably remember carrying on perfectly happily without Facebook or Twitter linking you with friends and acquaintances. But you still had a desire for belongingness. Social media taps directly into this desire, and it's for this reason it's so popular. As social creatures, we place great value on being part of a community—it's central to our sense of self-worth and happiness. What we seek within our communities are positive emotional experiences. Social media fills this role beautifully—and also fills some of the lack of community we experience as a result of our mobile, work-driven societies.

Within Pinterest you will express positive emotional experiences through the images you pin. The stronger your images are and the more deeply they tap into universal themes, the stronger the emotional connection from viewers. These repeated good feelings will cause followers to trust you and extend that emotional connection to your brand and products and services. The stronger the connections, the more sales and referrals.

What's important here for the purposes of this book is the cycle that's created—the social cycle. It can be broken down into three stages: emotional connection, sales, and advocates.

Let's examine each of these stages individually:

- **Emotional connection.** In the first stage an emotional connection is created by pinning and repinning images that speak to a set group of people. You may not even fully realize who these people are or where they live. They may just come to you like the Midwestern moms and Mormons did to Ben Silbermann in the early days of Pinterest. But an emotional connection is created, and it leads to the next stage.

- **Sales.** As people grow to trust you as a provider of ideas and inspiration, more referral traffic will arrive at your website or blog, and you will see an increase in sales. You will have solved a problem or fulfilled a desire for your clients. Following this, the emotional connection becomes even stronger. They've put money on it. If they're happy with your product, you will have moved to the next stage.

- **The creation of advocates.** Now you have followers who are emotionally bonded to you and your product or service. This is the best of all worlds. These advocates will in turn pin and repin your images and begin the process of creating an emotional connection in new people. These people will bring you more sales and tell their friends and connections. The cycle is complete.

This is all great in theory, you may say, but how do we apply it today to improve our businesses through Pinterest? By understanding that in the beginning especially, it's your job to oil the gears of the social cycle. It won't happen by its little ol' self. You need to get in there and become a socially active member of this new community. Your presence and actions will get those first people emotionally connected and buying. Fortunately, at Pinterest it's easy.

Let's look at how you can facilitate the social cycle.

A Most Common Mistake

To start with, let's dodge some dirt. There's a most common mistake in marketing your business with Pinterest, but it's an easy one to fix. Users of YouTube may have experienced the same issue. The key to social media lies in the word *social*. If you treat your Pinterest experience as just a place to store images, you're missing a massive advantage: the social advantage.

Yet if you approach Pinterest as a place to find and bond with potential clients, you will have an altogether different experience—an immensely positive one. The key is in thinking of Pinterest as a community. Within this community you can connect with prospective clients and get to know them while they get to know you. And all the time, you're sharing images and videos of things you love and are inspired by. Treat the Pinterest community as a place where you can trigger the social cycle.

As you develop more followers, they will learn to trust you and see value in your products or services. As they begin to buy them, they turn into your advocates. These advocates then start the cycle all over on your behalf. But don't make the mistake of thinking all you have to do is upload a bunch of images. You must become a valued member of your community. You must grease the wheels.

Maximizing the Social Elements of Pinterest

Four key elements will facilitate your activity as a member of your Pinterest community: repin, like, comment, and follow. We've already discussed these briefly, but now it's time to have a closer look.

Repin

As we mentioned previously, approximately 80 percent of Pinterest images are actually repins. It's a wonderful compliment to have your content repinned, because each time it's repinned, it ends up on that person's pinboard. In effect, the person is saying, "This is so good, I want to keep some for myself."

Don't ever be afraid to repin something in your niche that doesn't come from you and your business. Sharing ideas is the spirit of Pinterest. You're in the process of becoming a trusted resource, and this means providing ideas and inspiration from everywhere, not just your own corner store. With repinning you win twice: first, by complimenting the person you repinned from and, second, by sharing yet another great idea and image.

Like

This function works the same as it does on Facebook. Liking a pin gives a virtual thumbs-up to the pinner. Use this often. When people repin your content, like the repin in return. You're telling them you like the pin (your pin) and you like the fact they repinned it. Then like some more of their content. Return the social goodwill. It would be hard to overuse this simple yet effective tool.

Figure 7.1 Share your Pinterest pinboards with your Facebook fans.

TRAFFIC TIP

An excellent sharing tool between Facebook and Pinterest is built into your pinboards, as in Figure 7.1. Click on your pinboard, and you will see, next to the Title, the Facebook Like button. Click here, fill in a message to your Facebook fans, and click Post to Facebook. Now the images on the entire pinboard will be shared with your Facebook fans via a link along with your comment.

Comment

When people repin your content, another great way to engage them socially is to comment on their repin. "Thanks for sharing this information, much appreciated" will go a long way. This does the obvious job of thanking the person for sharing the pin, but it also creates a closer connection between you and the pinner. As well, visitors to that pin will see your name and realize you are the originator of the content. It all adds up.

Follow

The highest accolade on Pinterest is to follow people. This says you're interested in them and what they have to offer. Follow people who have the same niches, hobbies, or interests that you do. When you see that someone has started following you, click on the person's name and visit the Profile page. Check out who your followers are, and like, comment, or follow one or more of their boards in return. These are all ways to say thank you, and those are two mighty powerful words.

Keeping Track of Social Traffic

A variety of ways exist for you to see what kind of activity you're kicking up. First, Pinterest will send you an e-mail each time someone likes, repins, comments, or follows you and your images. This is great at the beginning because you can click on the user name of each person and like, repin, comment, or follow in return. However, as your community grows, the quantity of e-mails will become a bit of a pain. One option is to open a new e-mail account for just these e-mails. You can then go in once a day or a few times a week, whatever suits you, and see who's been doing what.

You also have the option to tailor your e-mails from Pinterest. Hover your mouse over your picture in the upper right-hand corner of any page. Click on Settings from the drop-down menu. Then click on Change Email Settings. From here you can choose which e-mails you want to receive and how often. Perhaps consolidating them into a weekly e-mail digest will serve the dual purposes of managing the traffic while still keeping you up to date with your likes, comments, etc.

On the left-hand side of the Pinners You Follow page is a Recent Activity box tallying the last 15 repins, likes, etc., done from your content. Again, this is fine when you're just starting, but as you get busier, you might miss good opportunities to create connections. If you stick with just this level of monitoring, be sure and check your Pinterest page frequently so you're able to respond appropriately.

For those people who want to track the referral traffic coming into their website from Pinterest—a very useful and exciting metric, indeed—Google Analytics provides a great service for just this. You can see exactly how much traffic is coming to your site from each individual pin or from Pinterest as a whole. (See Figure 7.2.) If you compare this with

	Referral Path		Visits ↓	Pages/Visit	Avg. Visit Duration	% New Visits
⊟	1. /pin/157906416/	⟐	203	4.19	00:00:19	0.49%
⊟	2. /pin/205687907951089844/	⟐	184	1.67	00:02:41	0.00%
⊟	3. /pin/43206477644764656/	⟐	111	4.10	00:04:16	14.41%
⊟	4. /pin/182606959860640047/	⟐	87	3.11	00:02:07	44.83%
⊟	5. /cinnamonmiles/american-girl-doll/	⟐	86	5.14	00:05:22	16.28%
⊟	6. /pin/104356916334964273/	⟐	86	3.45	00:01:40	60.47%
⊟	7. /pin/148478118934402957/	⟐	73	3.55	00:03:04	78.08%
⊟	8. /pin/43206477644807054/	⟐	65	3.12	00:02:01	24.62%
⊟	9. /pin/190206784231734082/	⟐	63	3.25	00:04:08	7.94%
⊟	10. /pin/43206477644742376/	⟐	58	5.97	00:04:16	13.79%

Figure 7.2 Google Analytics lets you see how many people visited your website from each Pinterest pin.

traffic from other social media sites, you learn who, in fact, is buttering the bread. So far, Google Analytics provides the most comprehensive view of what's happening between your website and Pinterest. If you don't have this feature yet, just Google it and then go through the installation process. It's easy and free. For more information on tracking tools, see Chapter 19.

Pinterest itself has a feature that allows you to find people who have pinned content from your website. This information is crucial because you can see exactly who is doing the pinning and you can connect with these people via commenting, repinning, liking, and following.

Two ways exist to access this information. Go to http://www.pinterest .com/source/your website address here. This will show you which images are being pinned from your blog or website.

Or click on any of your pins. Scroll down past the Comments area until you see Pinned via Pinmarklet from. Beneath this will be the name of your original website or blog. Click on this name, and you can see who is pinning what from the original source. When you see the people who are pinning from your website, make sure you develop a connection with them. (See Figure 7.3.)

Figure 7.3 The incoming pins from Jason's MarketingOnPinterest.com.

The difference between this tool and Google Analytics is that the latter will show you pins and repins from Pinterest to your website or blog. The Pinterest feature works in the opposite direction and in a more limited way—original pins only, from your website to Pinterest.

One more way to keep track of your Pinterest activity is to use outside tracking services. Many Pinterest users swear by these. Check out Pintics, Pinpuff, Pin Reach, and Curalate (see Chapter 19).

The Three Ps of the Pinterest Social Cycle

When used properly, the Pinterest community is a vast resource of potential clients and new business. If you become an active participant, spreading not only your message but that of others, you will reap attractive rewards. Let's look at it in summary.

Principle. As you emotionally engage your viewers through your images and Pinterest activity, a personal connection and trust will develop. Some of these relationships will convert into sales. The people who purchase your products or services will then turn into advocates who, through the process of repinning and commenting, will engage new viewers on your behalf.

Practice. Get involved with the four social elements of Pinterest. Raving fans don't just sprout up for no reason. Actively use the like, comment, repin, and follow functions to create relationships and goodwill. Track the key people who visit your website or blog and pin your original content directly onto Pinterest. When you can, create relationships with these people through the four social elements.

Profit. From within this community of people with shared interests and passions will arise not only more sales but also more advocates of your products who will market them within the Pinterest community and elsewhere. These advocates and the people within their influence will lead to many more sales. It's social contagion in action.

Weaving Pinterest into Your Social Media Marketing

*T*wenty years after its introduction, Microsoft Office Suite still dominates the home and business software scene. Microsoft Word documents are the everyday norm for writing of most any kind, and Excel and PowerPoint are standards for crunching numbers and displaying information. With accurate foresight, the Microsoft designers and programmers made sure the three applications worked together. Charts, graphics, and text can in many instances be interchanged among the three. Whether running a corporation or managing a home office, these three applications allow business and creative endeavors to run smoothly.

Social media can be thought of in the same interrelated way, especially when used in combination with the backbone of your marketing presence—your website or blog and e-mail address lists. From home-based start-ups to Fortune 500 behemoths, most businesses have a social media presence; yet a recent study by Insites Consulting found that only 16 percent felt they had fully integrated their social media presences. This despite the fact that the same study found integrated social media has three key benefits: marketing communications are more effective, customers are happier, and profits go up.

The message couldn't be clearer. Weaving Pinterest into your other social media outlets, whichever ones they may be, is essential in boosting customer satisfaction and profits. Like Microsoft's Office Suite program, when these features are optimized and function together, the result for your small business is increased efficiency, growth, and profits. Each social media platform works to enhance your website traffic and list of e-mail addresses for your newsletter. A very fine team indeed.

Tailoring Your Social Media Mix

So many options exist for social media, you could spend several days each week on their management. When not used efficiently and within an overall marketing plan, they turn into time vampires, dementedly sucking away precious hours that otherwise could actually be spent on running your business. The key is to use only those platforms that lead you most effectively to your end goal: creating an emotional connection with your followers that will lead to sales.

Which social media networks, then, will work best for you? It depends on your specific situation and personality. Each of these outlets has a different set of strengths and weaknesses, and each can be used in a different way to facilitate the same goal. By understanding your options and what each will do for you, you'll be able to choose the suite that works best for your unique business.

What you don't want to do is stretch yourself too thin within the social media world. It's better to go with fewer and run deep. Part of this is a factor of time. Each network has its own set of marketing functions that need to be nurtured and managed. If you have the time to run five or six, that's great; but if not, it's better to run two or three well, rather than miss out on opportunities through lack of an engaged and active presence. As well, depending on where you are already with your business, consider utilizing just a couple and then add more gradually. This way you can make sure they integrate fully, and if not, you haven't wasted too much time if you delete one and choose another.

Describing his own experiences, Jason traces the thought process he went through:

In considering how to market *Pinterest Power* through social media while still holding a full-time job at the university, I had to take into account the limited amount of time and energy available. In the end I decided on a combination of my MarketingOnPinterest blog, videos, and tutorials; Pinterest (of course); and my Twitter account. This combination made the most sense given the set of circumstances. We're actually debating whether or not to have a Facebook fan page because of the time it will take to sustain the ongoing conversations. We'll see, but each business must make these real-world decisions.

The key questions to ask are these: How will this or that social media network help me? What will it do for me, either alone or in combination with another network, that will help my business grow with the most impact? And how will each option increase traffic back to my website? Before you can answer these questions, you need to understand what your options are.

A Social Media Smorgasbord

Below is a down-and-dirty overview of the most prominent social media networks. We begin with a list of questions to ask regarding each one. These will help you clarify their business potential and weavability with other networks. You may be utilizing different social media sites from those mentioned here. If they're working well, that's great. Ask the same questions and determine how you can integrate them into your overall social media marketing suite.

Remember, if you have a social media outlet like Facebook, for example, where you already have a gazillion followers, consider it a given you'll be including it in your marketing plan.

To determine if a social media network is an optimal one for your business, ask yourself:

- How much time will I need to spend daily or weekly?

- What results do I expect from this time spent over the short, medium, and long term?

- How will this enhance traffic back to my website or blog?

- Will I be able to grow my e-mail address list from this source?

- How much presence do I have here already, or am I starting from zero?

- Will I be able to exchange information between this network and the other(s) I'm using? For example, can I easily place Follow Me On . . . buttons, have links to articles, share appealing images and videos, etc.?

- Am I comfortable with this form of media? Would I enjoy spending time here and connecting with new people?

Now, let's have a look at the smorgasbord of goodies we get to choose from.

Facebook

This is the granddaddy of them all. With over 845 million users (per Wikipedia, February 2012) and still growing, this is the site that comes to mind when we hear about social media. Chances are you have an account already and at least use it for personal purposes. Facebook works best at facilitating conversations with your fans. Check out Facebook's advertising program (http://www.facebook.com/about/ads) to help you grow this number.

The downside of Facebook is that it's time consuming. You must continually make new posts and respond to people's replies and posts. If you're not able to make the commitment to add new content and communicate with others several times a week, then you won't be optimizing this platform. InsideFacebook (http://www.insidefacebook.com) is a clever blog that helps keep you up to date with all the various gizmos and changes.

Twitter

It's estimated that 1.6 billion search queries are conducted *per day* on Twitter. That's nearly a quarter of the population of the earth—every day. Clearly, Twitter carries significant reach. And if you think about it, Twitter is similar to Pinterest, while at the same time being opposite.

Whereas on Pinterest we pin hundreds and even thousands of images and videos, with Twitter we "microblog." That is, we send frequent small updates via text, not images. And within these differences lies opportunity. You can reach new people via an alternative medium.

YouTube

Many of us know YouTube as that service that has all those crazy videos we get sent via e-mail. Yes, 'tis the same creature, but it can also be an effective marketing tool for your small business. Making your own videos is a bit time consuming but can be a great way for your followers to get to know you better. YouTube videos can easily be shared among YouTube, Facebook, and Pinterest.

The downside of YouTube is that it's fairly labor intensive. Yes, you can do informal work, but to create professional-looking videos takes time and equipment.

LinkedIn

This site leads the ranks in business-related social media. Businesspeople use LinkedIn to stay connected, exchange industry-related information, and even find new jobs. If your Pinterest niche has a business-related aspect, like being a writer, lawyer, life coach, etc., then you should consider this site. For more information on using Pinterest to expand your service-oriented businesses, see Chapter 13.

Google+

This platform is new to the scene and behaves much the same way as Facebook. You develop circles of people, can share activities and conversations, and can even have live Google chats with several people at a time. If you're already established on Facebook, you may not need Google+ added to your mix. In fact, some people have suggested it's actually a ghost town when it comes to active participation, the idea being it's too similar to Facebook. It would seem the jury's still out about whether this is an efficient social media platform.

Yelp and Foursquare

These two platforms are set up to exchange information within specific geographic areas. If your niche has a local aspect to it, you may well consider adding these to your suite. If you're exhibiting your wares in local craft or art fairs, or perhaps have a yoga studio or gourmet food store, these might be a good addition.

Tying in a Blog and Newsletter

At the core of your marketing endeavor sits the all-important website from which sales are made. Every other tool orbits this life-sustaining sun. However, some orbit closer to the sun, and therefore have more impact, and others orbit farther away, with less influence. Closest to the sun rotate the blog and e-mail newsletter. As you'll see in Chapter 11, it's not uncommon to use the blog itself as your business center.

Often, the blog is where you educate, entertain, and have conversations with your followers and clients. You can link it directly to your main website and also provide links for your Facebook fans, YouTube subscribers, LinkedIn contacts, and Pinterest followers. The blog's focus shouldn't just be on product; rather it's more powerful as a place for customers to go and learn. Provide tutorials, educational articles, how-to videos, competitions, and even drawings to inspire, educate, and activate your clients. Tie all these into your presence on Pinterest, and you'll attract many new followers and their friends and contacts.

It's also powerful to reveal more about yourself within your blog along with your views of the world. You can get personal. Here you build up your expertise in real time, as a real person. This works as a complement to your website, which is more business oriented. It also fits in with Pinterest, where you have business-oriented images, as well as a collection of personal ones. Remember, the end goal is to emotionally engage viewers and potential clients. Part of how we do this is by letting them know who we are as individuals.

Next, and for many the most important online activity you can conduct, is developing and growing an e-mail address list. One powerful option is to develop a newsletter to go along with your e-mail list, and it isn't as daunting as it might first seem. Monthly or bimonthly is fine, and some of the content can be blog-related material that proved most popular. As well, include special deals, product promotions, and any other hot-and-heavy news that needs to get out. While social media sites may come and go, e-mail is still the most common form of Internet communication. You connect directly with your customers, rather than hoping they come to you. See Chapter 16 for more on building your e-mail list.

Certain service providers will help you organize your e-mail list and marketing endeavors. MailChimp offers a guide for explaining its services to online sellers. Those businesses focused on information products (i.e., that sell information—examples include investment advice, recipes, market research, and online classes) prefer Aweber software for its advanced functionality features. And Constant Contact offers a solid product with excellent training.

One Step at a Time

As you consider these various options, resist the temptation to be completely overwhelmed and therefore stunned into inaction. Rather, go back to the core goal: getting people emotionally engaged so that they come to your website and buy things.

Remember what you learned in Chapter 3: start small, think big, and be patient. Understand your options, have goals in mind, and then take one small step at a time, making sure you're comfortable and enjoying the ride along the way. If this means only having a blog and a Pinterest account, great! Work with that. Use the tools we provide that apply. Over time you may want to add a Facebook presence, or create a website, or start collecting e-mail addresses for a newsletter. You can do all of it, but you don't have to do any of it. You don't want your small business to start turning into something that sounds like hard work. The hours you put in may be long, but if you love what you're doing, they'll fly by fast and in good company.

Weaving It All Together

Now comes the fun part. You understand your social media options and have made an initial selection of those that will work well with Pinterest and your other marketing endeavors. You've revived yourself after the dizzy-from-too-many-options stage, and you've decided to take it one step at a time within your comfort level.

So just how do we go about getting all these separate platforms and projects to weave together and make the whole greater than the sum of the parts? Below we list seven keys for doing just this. Some will apply now; some won't yet but may down the road. Each will have a direct impact on getting more engagement from your clients and contacts and therefore get more traffic to your website.

1. Maintain Your Presence

Think of this as the most important key and one that will be crucial in determining which platforms you end up utilizing. Social media doesn't work if you don't become and stay an active member of your community. Therefore, only choose those that you're willing to make a daily or at least weekly time commitment to.

2. Use Social Media Buttons

These are those little square symbols that allow us to access different social media platforms. You see them often at the very top of a website, blog, or article. At the most basic level, these allow your potential clients to communicate or follow you on the social media platform of their choice. Make sure you use these buttons everywhere you can. Getting people to follow you on your other social media sites will increase exposure and eventually get them to Pinterest and your website, even if they take the scenic route.

TRAFFIC TIP

Add Pinterest Pin It buttons to all your website or blog pages and images. Then use calls to action by adding text such as "Pin this photo [or article or DIY tip] if you like it!" Tell people what to do, and you'll get more pins.

As well, use Share buttons. Make it easy for your clients and followers to share the great ideas they've found through you. Facebook has the Like It button, and Pinterest has the Pin It button. Add these to the product pages in your website or blog. Encourage viewers to share your articles, images, and other content. These valuable buttons allow for seamless sharing and recommendation of your product or service. Best of all, your clients do it for you. Once again, you get advocates going to work for you.

3. Integrate Your Material

For example, if you can run your Twitter feed within your Facebook page, blog, or website, do so. This will encourage viewers not only to read your tweets, but, you hope, to follow you on Twitter. The more exposure you get, the better, because through each vehicle you'll gently be reminding viewers of your Pinterest profile and your product or service.

If you write an article, see where else you can post it other than on your blog. How about on Pinterest, Facebook, and LinkedIn? This way, one article gets quadruple exposure.

4. Time Is Money

The more efficiently you use your social media, the bigger the bang you'll get for the amount of time you've spent. Automatic updates, or nearly automatic, will help enormously. You must determine which site will update to which other site, as these will vary.

Here's one example of a nearly automated routine: Take a blog article, image, or piece of content. Pin it to Pinterest. Bring up the pin, and on the right-hand side, tweet it. With one more click, like it to Facebook. From your blog to three other platforms, with just a few clicks—that's time efficient.

If you're using YouTube and videos, here's another example. Take a new video you've created and embed it in your blog. Pin that blog to Pinterest. Then tweet it as you did above and again like it to Facebook. Finally, you can have your LinkedIn profile automatically updated by your blog, and so the new video content will be updated to LinkedIn. Whew! Not bad exposure for one video.

5. Stay Up to Date

Technology seems to change at the speed of light, and social media is no exception. Take time to read articles on the platforms you've chosen, watch for new features and additions, and in general try to be on top of at least those areas of technology your business is counting on. This doesn't need to be a time-consuming endeavor, but it does need to be a regular one. You don't want to miss out on new opportunities or find you're working in last year's program that's now nearly obsolete.

6. Analyze!

Use Google Analytics to study which social media outlets are sending you the most business. Understand what's happening at the deepest level of your marketing plan so that you can act to make any changes necessary. If something is working really well, do more of it. If you're wasting your time in another area, well, the answer is clear there too: change or delete it. If you don't measure your progress, you won't be able to understand it and reap the maximum benefits.

7. Don't Overdo It

Two reasons exist for this. One, if you're not active on a social media platform, you're wasting your time. Time is money. Two, don't get burned out. If you're hustling trying to manage seven different platforms and

TRAFFIC TIP

Pinterest is one of the most time-efficient social media sites available. The reason for this? The repin. When you post images that inspire viewers, repinning takes over and the work is out of your hands. Remember in Chapter 5 we noted that Liz Marie Galvan had her craft idea pinned over 22,000 times (Figure 5.1)? She only made the blog post once. That's time efficient. Keep in mind that Pinterest itself is one of your most effective social media tools.

integrating all the new material and maintaining and initiating conversations, you won't have time to recharge your batteries and actually enjoy what you're doing. Chances are your family will miss you too. Marketing done properly will leverage your time with the express goal of increasing business. Focus, analyze, and by all means stop and smell the virtual roses.

The Three Ps of Social Media

Principle. Social media can be used effectively to grow your small business. By weaving these platforms together, including at the forefront Pinterest, you will leverage the overall returns. These returns include better communication, happier clients, and more sales.

Practice. Start by studying the various social media options available and determining which will work best in your situation. Then follow the seven keys above to integrate them to save time and increase exposure.

Profit. The increased exposure you achieve through your social media marketing efforts will lead to more traffic to both Pinterest and your website. This will lead to more sales. Once again, the line is direct.

Pin Tips and Contests

*A*ll the pins, videos, likes, and comments won't get you anywhere if the viewer doesn't eventually click on the Pinterest image and go to your website. Herein resides the nut of the issue, because from here is where sales are made. Unfortunately, no one panacea exists to achieve this feat. Heck, it wouldn't be fun if it were easy, would it? Rather, the miracle of increased sales occurs over a period of time and after layers of carefully thought-out marketing strategies.

Part of the equation lies in good practices: know your target market inside and out, use solid pinning and linking techniques, and pay attention to typical Pinterest users' behavior patterns. Add proven marketing campaigns to these practices, and over time patterns will begin to appear. Giant arcs will form like transatlantic flight patterns, from your social media platforms to Pinterest, from Pinterest to your website, from your website back to Pinterest and other social media. The ever-increasing flow of traffic will lead to the magic last step: more clicks on your website pages and therefore more sales.

This chapter will cover some of the best practices involved in making sure traffic finds its way to your site through little-known tips and the magic of creative contests. Carefully study the strategies involved and nurture the ones that suit your situation.

It's Midnight on Wednesday. It Must Be Time to Pin!

Sounds crazy? Maybe, but more than one study has shown certain times and days are better for social media activity than others. Before we go into the details and how you can utilize the data, first remember there are no absolutes in this type of general research. What works for one person may completely bomb with another. The key is to diligently keep trying to understand who your prospective clients are and how best to communicate with them. It's easy to brush off data like these as too far out there, but you could be missing a grand opportunity. Understand, try, and then judge. That's the formula that will pay off best in the end.

TRAFFIC TIP

In Jason's experience: In the first four months of our company's presence on Pinterest, we received just over 2,000 repins with referral links back to the website. We also received over 7,000 actual visits to our website from Pinterest. This means a 3:1 ratio of website visits per repin is reasonable and even conservative. For every repin, we can now estimate we'll receive at least three website visits. While your results will undoubtedly vary from ours, over time you'll learn to identify your site's traffic patterns and to depend on them to grow your business.

Part of the beauty of blogs, e-commerce sites, and social media networks is that they generate an enormous amount of data. Fortunately for the Pinterest marketer, some people can't wait for Saturday afternoon to roll around so they can crunch these data into meaningful trends and patterns. However, given Pinterest's relatively short life span to date, not as much Pinterest-specific information exists. Most social media data available pertain to blogs, Twitter, Facebook, and LinkedIn. But we can still learn from this information and the Pinterest data that are trickling in. Analyzing user behavior is an underutilized tool for marketers.

So let's start by looking at what Dan Zarrella, social media scientist for HubSpot, has found:

1. Data on Twitter showed that tweets done at 4 p.m. EST received the most amount of retweets.

2. Fridays are the best day to tweet and get retweeted.

3. Articles posted on Facebook are shared more often when they're posted on Saturdays and Sundays.

4. The best time of day for posting articles on Facebook was 9 a.m. EST.

5. Most blogs are read in the morning, almost twice as many as are read at night.

Okay, how do we transfer this knowledge into helping us with our Pinterest marketing? First, the obvious. If you're using Twitter or Facebook and blogging for your social media efforts, give the above data a try and see what happens. The risk in timing your communication to fit these trends is minimal to nonexistent, and the reward might be interesting. Second, if trends exist for other social media results, why would Pinterest be any different? As humans we're creatures of habit, no matter the platform. Analysis on Pinterest has actually found just this. Similar trends appear on close inspection. Have a look at the following:

- The best times to pin on Pinterest are between 2 and 4 p.m. and between 8 p.m. and 1 a.m. EST. (By "best times" we mean the times that give you an edge on the number of repins.)

- The best day to pin is Saturday, and the second best is Wednesday.

- However, according to Bit.ly.com's chief scientist, Hilary Mason, the best time to pin is Saturday morning. (Bit.ly.com is known for helping clients to shorten their URLs and to track and analyze website traffic.)

So while there's some variance in data, patterns have emerged. Let's take this one step further, assuming these times really are effective for gaining more repins, and understand how this could affect your bottom line.

Scenario One

You pin an attractive image from your website at a nonpeak time and get 10 repins. Each of those repins then gets 10 repins. You're up to 110 repins in total. Now, let's say each of those 110 repins gets repinned 10 times. Your total is 1,100 new repins plus the 110 they were pinned from. This makes 1,210 repins. If we use the data from the Traffic Tip shown earlier in the chapter, it's not unrealistic to expect three visits to your website for every one repin. You could expect 3,630 new clicks to your website. Not bad, considering all you did was pin a great image to begin with.

Scenario Two

You pin the same attractive image but at the peak time of midnight on Saturday. Let's assume all you get is a 10 percent increase in repinning activity and only on that first image you pinned at midnight. We can't know what time the repins were done, so let's assume they were at nonpeak times. So instead of 10 repins on that first image, you get 11. Each of those 11 original repins was then repinned 10 times. This sums to 110 repins plus the original 11 repins for 121 in total. Now, each of those is repinned 10 times. You have 1,210 new repins plus the 121 they were repinned from. This totals 1,331 repins from the single image. Times this by three website visits per repin, and you end up with the potential for 3,993 new website clicks. By posting your image at a peak time and with only one extra repin as a result, after three generations of repinning you increased your potential website hits by 363, or roughly 10 percent.

If you keep extrapolating these numbers, it's easy to see that if you get a hot image being repinned, it would be significantly in your favor to have posted it at a peak time.

One more arrow in your marketing quiver!

Optimal Frequency and Quantity of Pinning

How often and how much should you pin to get the maximum quality and quantity of responses? Dos and don'ts exist that will get you into good habits from the beginning and ensure a smooth progression into steady referral traffic.

First of all, don't info-dump. Especially when you first start on Pinterest, it can be tempting to take all those great images you've accumulated of exotic ducks over the years and pin every one of them during one marathon pinning session. You'll end up with a beautiful pinboard, no doubt, but what kind of experience are you providing for your followers?

First, on that one pinning day, your followers' Pinners You Follow page will be crammed with your duck pictures. This behavior can easily teeter from interesting to annoying. Second, in order to reward your duck pinboard followers, you need to keep pinning duck images. That's why they're following you. If you post them all on day one, you'll have nothing left to share with them later.

A better alternative is to trickle out your images over time. Pin one or two images a day, and do this regularly. Gradually, you can branch out into new but related boards, such as "Classic Habitats," "Nature Images," "Bird Photography Tips," or even "Duck Hunting Gear and Techniques" if that's your direction. With this gentle approach and steady output of information, you build up a reputation with your followers as a trusted resource. This trust leads to more referral traffic to your website or blog.

So just how much should you pin? As with most social media sites, the more active you are, the better the long-term results. Frequently and regularly pinning great images will get you more likes, comments, repins, and followers through the sheer math of it all. When you have fewer boards, you'll pin fewer images. But as the number of boards increases and you want to reward your followers, you'll develop a steady pinning practice.

Choose those boards with the most followers and pin at least three to four images a week. For those boards that you want to grow the number of followers on, try a pin or two a day. Through trial and error you will reach the fine balance of enough pinning to keep the followers growing, but yet not so much that you spend too much time pinning.

Pinning infrequently gives subpar results, as does info dumping. It's most effective to pin great images regularly and consistently over time. People will follow you because they know what they're going to get and they like it. You'll be exposing them to beautiful images and all the while educating them about what they love and about your brand. Again, this will lead to an increase in referral traffic to your website.

Links to Last

As you become more familiar with Pinterest, you'll notice that some pins and repins don't link back to the original website. What's up with that? A very good question, indeed. In order to drive traffic to your website, it's critical that a link exist within the Pinterest image. Unfortunately, through multiple generations of repinning, the links can get removed or changed.

On Pinterest five locations exist for placing the URL so that it links or directs the viewer to your website.

1. Linked to the pinned image itself. This happens automatically when you pin the image from the source, i.e., your blog or website.

2. Within the pin description. This is a powerful tool if you also combine it with a call to action, such as "Click here for 20 slimming summer salad recipes!"

3. In the tagline. On your Profile page you can place your website in the tagline along with who you are and your message.

4. In the comments section of any pin.

5. On your images. Place your logo, brand, and website name directly on your images through Photoshop. The link may get lost over time, but the image will always retain your site name and brand.

The first and most obvious way to ensure that your images have a link back to your site is to pin the image from that original source. If you're not sure if you've done it properly, just click on the image and see where it takes you. By taking care to pin the image right in the first place, you avoid many problem issues. If you do see one of your images repinned without a link to your website, simply leave a comment thanking the person for sharing it and add your link there. It's not ideal, but it's the best you can do in that situation.

One potential source of trouble arises if you upload an image from your personal computer, as we mentioned in Chapter 5. When pins are made this way, there's no link included. To rectify this you must go in and manually add a link, which is time consuming. A far better solution is to post the image on your blog or website first and then pin it from

TRAFFIC TIP

When you pin an image from your site, make sure you pin it from the exact page the content is posted on. You want the links as deep inside your site as possible so don't link the image back to the general welcome page. If your image sits on the fifth page of a long series of kitchen sink samples, make sure the link takes the viewers to that specific page with the sink you pinned. This way, if they want to purchase it or become more deeply involved, they're right there and don't have to go searching.

there with your site link attached. Once you've pinned it, you can like it on Facebook, tweet it, or integrate it with any of your other social media efforts.

Finally, the best way to ensure that your brand, logo, and website stay attached to your images is to add them to the image itself with Photoshop. This may take a little time to gain the know-how, but nothing too daunting. You'll end up with an image that ensures your marketing message with or without the link. See Figure 9.1 for a great example by Courtney Slazinic of clickitupanotch.com. Notice how she has an attractive logo that doesn't distract from the image, but rather adds her personal style to it.

Composition: Rule of Thirds
www.click it up a notch.com

Figure 9.1 Use Photoshop to add a logo and website name to an image. The pinner here began with the title of the pin, followed by her details. (http://www.click itupanotch.com)

Contests

Conducting contests on Pinterest is proving to be a great way to increase traffic to your pinboards and to energize existing followers. An example of this is ModCloth's contest in Chapter 2. Word spreads of the contest and potential prize, and people get caught up in the spirit of competition. All these qualities lead directly to more traffic back to your original blog or website. Before you begin any contest, make sure you look into Pinterest's current terms of service. This will give you the latest on Pinterest's rules regarding running contests through the Pinterest website.

We asked Pinterest directly about contests:

Q. We write about conducting contests on Pinterest in the book and include examples of nicely designed contests, such as the recent Pottery Barn Teens contest [see Figure 9.2] and the ModCloth contest. What's Pinterest's perspective on contests being conducted on the platform? Will it be a viable marketing option for the long term, or is Pinterest considering going the way of Facebook and Google+ and banning them?

A. Pinterest is a growing service and company, so product-changes and emerging policies will definitely influence marketers or promotions in the future. However, staying aligned with our Pin Etiquette will probably always inform a "nicely designed" contest on Pinterest.

For instance, a contest that asks entrants to engage in genuine user-activities—like creating a board filled with things that inspire them, centered around a theme—are probably more memorable and fun for Pinners compared to contests which simply ask people to comment or re-pin within a certain amount of time.

Many types of contests exist, and you can tailor your own to suit your niche, personality, and experience. Within them all, however, are a few best practices you'll be wise to follow:

- Read up to check for the latest Pinterest rules regarding contests and competitions. Currently there aren't any, but things can change and it's best to stay informed.

ARE YOU ON
Pinterest?

Enter our contest and
you could win a $1,000
gift card or one of five
$100 gift cards!

Enter by
March 22nd ▸

● Follow @PBTEEN on Pinterest

● Create a board titled "PBteen Dream Room Inspiration"

● Pin at least five PBteen items that inspire your dream room,
and in the comments of each pin, add #PBTEEN

● When your board is complete, post a comment on our pin with a link to
your board

Get Started ▸

Figure 9.2 Pottery Barn Teen ran this simple contest on Pinterest.

- Create a visually enticing contest pin that clearly states you're running a contest and specifies what the rules are. Pin this image onto a contest pinboard. If you can't fit all the rules on the image, refer the viewer to your website or blog that the image will be linked to. Make sure the pin is attractive and will be a natural for repinning. See Figure 9.2 for a great example of a contest pin.

- For the contest itself, ask your participants to create something that will end up promoting your images and brand. In the end, contests are marketing exercises. Keep this in mind as you create yours.

- Set clear start and end dates on the contest pin and your blog or website.

- Choose a compelling prize that fits the target market for the contest. Everybody loves a prize, so think hard about this and choose an enticing one. Consider giving prizes to more than one person or making a top 10 list. Everyone loves a bit of attention and appreciation.

- Clearly state on your pinboard and site what constitutes an official entry. You don't want people thinking they've signed up but haven't. Avoid misunderstandings by communicating clearly in the beginning.

Below are four contest formats for you to choose from. Start with one of these or create your own.

Best Pinboard Contest

With this format you invite contestants to create a new pinboard filled with images from your website or Pinterest pinboards. Give the contest a theme that ties back to your products or services. For example, ask contestants to create a "Chocolate Nemesis" board, or "Best Prom Dress," or "Most Unusual Gardening Tips." Design the goal in line with the content you have available to pin from, and state that the contestants must pin from your pinboards, blog, or website. (A variation is to require only a certain number of pins to come from your site; the rest they can get creative with and choose from anywhere.) You then pick and announce the winner(s). Participants share their boards with one another by posting a comment on your main contest pin with a link back to their own board.

For this contest to work effectively, it's crucial that the images your contestants can choose to pin from are well branded. Use Photoshop to imprint your logo, brand, and website address on each image. You need to have your name and logo passed from one viewer to the next, as this is what will give you the most impact.

The Repin Contest

This varietal allows the participants to select the winner. Use the same setup as above where you pick the theme, and specify that a set number of pins must come from your branded material. The winner is then based on the board whose images receive the most amount of repins and likes from the general Pinterest public.

The Themed Giveaway Contest

Sunglass Warehouse ran this type of contest in early 2012. The company cleverly used a spring break theme and offered free sunglasses and Target gift cards as the prizes. Notice in Figure 9.3 how the individual participants had to pin 10 preselected images onto their boards. This ensured lots of repinning of those specific images, which most probably brought in a boon of referral traffic for Sunglass Warehouse.

How To Enter:

» Follow @Sunglass Warehouse on Pinterest (*Don't have a Pinterest account? Don't worry! You can request one in the comments below, or email Beth and she'll send you an invitation to join!*)

» Create a Pinterest board that shows off your personal Spring Break style and be sure to title it "SW Spring Break Style"

» Your board should include the 10 pins listed below. For each pin, include the contest category it belongs to along with our Pinterest handle – @Sunglass Warehouse & the hashtag #SWspringbreak in the description

» Once you've crafted the ultimate Spring Break board, send it our way by posting a link to the board in the comments section below

sunglass warehouse

SPRING BREAK STYLE
PINTEREST CONTEST

Enter to win:
2 pairs of sunglasses & a $50 Target gift card
for Spring Break 2012!

Figure 9.3 A successful themed contest run by Sunglass Warehouse.

Random Drawing Contest

Contests don't have to be difficult. Consignment Mommies created an effective yet simple random drawing contest with a side prize of the winner getting to choose a friend to win an extra gift card. In Figure 9.4 notice how the rules and requirements are clear and fun.

Win $100 in our Pin to Win Contest!

ConsignmentMommies.com is all about moms helping moms! So, to help spread the love & share some tips & advice, we're hosting a Pinterest-ing contest! You love consigning, you love Pinterest... combine the two and win!

How to Enter the Contest

- **Step 1:** Create Your Own Consignment Pinboard

- **Step 2:** Visit our ConsignmentMommies.com Contest Pinboard and repin 5 to 10 of your favorite ConsignmentMommies.com pins to your own pinboard.

- **Step 3:** Email pinterest@consignmentmommies.com with a link to your Pinboard to enter.

- **Step 4:** Encourage your friends to pin! If you win, you'll select one repinner to receive a $50 Gift Card!

Winner Selection:

At the close of the contest, we will select a random winner via Random.org. That winner will select another pinner to receive the "$50 Friend Gift Card." (note: friend winners must have participated in the contest). In the event that no "friends" have participated, you may choose someone at random.

Figure 9.4 A simple random drawing contest run by Consignment Mommies.

The Three Ps of Putting on Contests

Principle. Pinterest contests are a great way to energize existing clients, generate new followers, and increase referral traffic to your site.

Practice. Use one of the examples above to create your own contest. Create a clear contest pin explaining the rules, and place your logo, website, and brand on your images to be pinned.

Profit. The increased pinning and repinning from your site will turn right around and lead to more referral traffic to you, which will lead to more sales. In the process, you've created something fun for your clients and followers. This form of goodwill carries endless ramifications.

Driving and Growing Pinterest Traffic

B y now you are probably up and running on Pinterest and achieving some level of success. You're pinning and repinning images, and others are doing the same with your content. The number of followers is trickling up, and life is fine. However, the goal of this book isn't to be fine; it's to be spectacular. Increasing business a bit is great, but how about making some real deep-seated changes instead. Lesser-known marketing strategies can work wonders at amping up your Pinterest experience.

To begin with, you will have noticed that some pins work better than others. They get repinned and liked much more frequently. Psychological, emotional, and intellectual reasons exist for this. When you understand these triggers, you will be able to create pins that appeal to those core motivating factors and get people clicking through to your website.

This brings us to the next point. Building a new social media network from scratch sounds like a lot of work, doesn't it? Wouldn't it be great if you could bring along your other communities, clients, and relationships to Pinterest? This way you could leverage the worlds you've already created into your Pinterest experience. Well, we'll show you how to do just this too. Read on!

Pins with Punch

The goal of every image you pin from your website is to get the viewer to click on it and be taken back to your website. It's only from here that he or she can actually purchase your product or service. So how do you create content that achieves this golden goal?

It all goes back to the DNA built into Pinterest. Ben Silbermann, one of the cofounders, spent time working at Google on the display ad team. Display ads are advertisements that website owners install on their websites to generate income. When viewers click on the ads, they're taken directly to the corresponding website. Companies and individuals pay for these ads, and fortunes have been amassed by correctly using marketing strategies associated with them.

If all this is sounding eerily familiar, you're right. Pinterest can actually be thought of as a giant display ad network. Used properly, it's capable of driving massive referral traffic back to your website. One crucial difference? It's absolutely free.

Let's look at how you can create an efficient selection of images that work as display ads. It all begins with the goal mentioned above: getting the viewer intrigued enough that she clicks on the pinned image and is taken back to your website. Because the concept of display ads isn't new—some of the key drivers go all the way back to print ads—we can learn from what's been done before.

Below we outline six of the most effective formulas for getting people clicking on your images.

Advertorials

This is an ad that's mixed with editorial content so it doesn't quite look like an ad. However, it positions you as an expert and provides useful information to the viewer. The attraction here is the educational nature of the pins. Viewers then repin to share what they've learned. Unique to Pinterest, the advertorial can be very long from top to bottom. Viewers simply keep scrolling down the page. If it were a newspaper ad, every extra inch would cost more money.

Infographics

This pin is a bit like the advertorial except it's more visually oriented. You're creating an image that conveys information the reader will benefit from. It's creatively displayed, often with humor, and piques the interest of the viewers because they quickly learn something. Pick a subject from your niche that you can create a teaching visual image from. This works well with both product sellers and service providers, and humor adds to the impact. (See Figure 10.1.) As with advertorials, infographics can be narrow and run a long way down the screen.

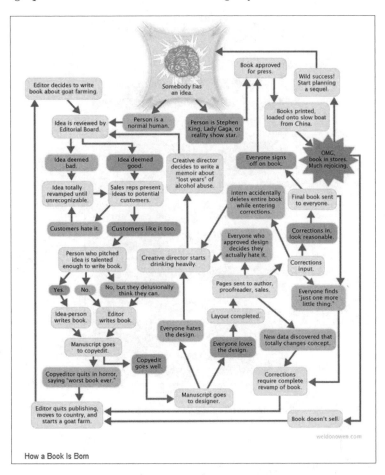

Figure 10.1 This humorous infographic from mediabistro.com is a great way to share information and stir interest in what else you might have to offer.

The How-To Pin

Sharing knowledge is a huge attraction for people on Pinterest. All it takes is a few minutes scrolling down the Popular page to see how many pins are how-to in nature. Take advantage of this by teaching viewers something about your niche. Whether it's a craft idea, gardening tip, or great new way to flatten those abs, create a how-to pin with step-by-step instructions. This can be done solely with visuals, or you can add text. Get creative, and people will respond with repins. (See Figure 10.2.)

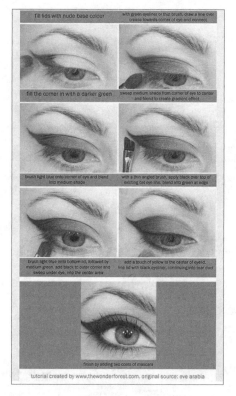

Figure 10.2 A clever how-to pin from www.thewonderforest.com (original source: eve arabia).

Curiosity-Driven Pins

Here you give the viewers an image or bit of information that intrigues them and therefore gets them to click through to your website to learn more. Only by going to your website will they get an answer to the question you've created. In a sense, all good pins do this, but the curiosity-driven pin just does it more directly, as in Figure 10.3.

Figure 10.3 An excellent example of a curiosity-driven pin by budgetsavvy diva.com.

Emotionally Engaging Pins

Again, this concept overlaps many of the other types of pins. When we're emotionally engaged, we want to get closer and learn more, and this leads to more clicks on the website link. Each of the pins you use should be emotionally engaging. However, you can also emphasize this emotional engagement directly, as encouragement to get the viewers to visit your website. Think about making your viewers laugh, cry, feel patriotic, feel spiritual, or feel proud to be part of a special group. The best way to then get them to follow through and click on your website link is to use this emotion-provoking image in relation to your product or service. (See Figure 10.4.)

WHAT TO DO WHEN YOUR KIDS CRY ?

Figure 10.4 This pin engages us emotionally with a powerful image. It then promises to give the viewer child-rearing advice (www.healthchildren.org).

Memes

These are those images, YouTube videos, and bits of humor that spread through our culture like wildfire. From babies biting fingers to cats boxing with raccoons, it's as if each week we get a new-flavored meme to entertain us. The views on them can reach the millions. We're not saying you should expect this type of result, but using humor with a picture, whether it relates to your niche or not, is a great way to get attention and followers. Just remember to be tasteful and not overdo it. (See Figure 10.5.)

I don't know how to say this, but...

you don't have a hamster anymore

Figure 10.5 A classic meme.

As with so many of the sets of tools you have to work with, the best way to approach these powerful pins is to try a few different styles and see which ones work best. Perhaps you're great with how-to but short on humor. Or the thought of creating an advertorial makes you want to shut yourself in your closet with the lights off, but yet those pictures of the kids from the family reunion have a dozen funny scenes you could turn into memes. What you choose to pin is personal and reveals who you are. Celebrate this, experiment with different ideas, and use what works.

Be sure to monitor your pins so you know what's getting attention. As we discussed in Chapter 7, use Google Analytics or one of the other tracking services to stay on top of your results. Only by taking the time to study the reaction that your images are getting will you know what to emphasize, adjust, or just plain throw out.

The Three Ps of Pins with Punch

Principle. The goal of your pinning efforts is to get the viewer to click on the pin and visit your website. After all, it's only from here that sales can be made. By pinning images that carry visual, intellectual, or emotional "hooks," you can facilitate this process.

Practice. Try creating each of the different types of pins we've covered in this chapter. Every one of them carries the potential to intrigue the viewers enough to get them to visit your site. Over time you will discover which types of pins are most natural for you and bring in the most referral traffic.

Profit. As your proficiency with pins grows, so will referral traffic to your site. The more traffic you get to your site, the more sales you will make. Fun, isn't it?

Driving Traffic to Your Pinterest Profile

So far in this chapter, we've discussed how to get more traffic to your website from Pinterest. Now it's time to flip that concept on its head. As any savvy Pinterest marketer knows, the more existing customers of yours you can send to Pinterest, the better for your business. "What?"

you might ask. "If they're already customers, why should I need to worry about sending them to Pinterest?"

Herein is the secret. One of the wisest social media strategies you can have is to drive traffic to your Pinterest profile. Think about it: when you invite someone, the first thing he or she does is follow you. Your current clients are already advocates of your product and services. So by getting clients, friends, and members of your other social media communities onto Pinterest, you have a built-in set of advocates. These people already know you and have an established level of trust. Logically, their first steps will be to comment, like, repin, and follow your images and boards. They will then share these with their friends and acquaintances. Each of these people becomes a prospective client. How cool is that?

ModCloth had over 140,000 pins onto Pinterest from its website in March 2012. In its words again:

> The majority of traffic we receive from Pinterest is user-generated, meaning our customer is pinning images from our website. Brands that prioritize publishing interesting photography and graphics that delight the Pinterest demographic base will see their content organically thrive on Pinterest.

Let's look at six effective ways you can generate traffic into Pinterest.

1. Use your Facebook page to mention Pinterest and share content. This can be your own or other people's content. The goal is to pique your fans' interest and get them to join. Offer to invite them to join.

2. On YouTube, create call-to-action overlays that ask people to follow you on Pinterest. This way, when people view your video, they can easily click on the link. The Help feature on YouTube will walk you through how to do this.

3. Post an article on your website or blog about the benefits of Pinterest. E-mail this same article to everyone on your business e-mail list. You can either write this yourself or post someone else's article while giving the person credit. People are already

hearing about Pinterest, so when they see you also mentioning it, this might be the final push they need to join. Make sure you offer to invite them.

Continue to write or post Pinterest articles periodically. You want to keep the idea in front of your readers but yet not bore or annoy them with too much hype.

4. Add the red Follow Me On Pinterest buttons to your other social media icons, such as those for Facebook, Twitter, and LinkedIn. Place these icons on the home page or profile of each form of social media, including e-commerce sites such as Etsy and Amazon.

5. If your website or blog runs on the WordPress platform, use the Hello Bar plug-in to create a call to action to follow you on Pinterest. Visit Hellobar.com for more information.

TRAFFIC TIP

When you see that people have repinned an image of yours, check out their profiles and see if you have other things in common. It's great community-building practice to thank them for their repin and ask them to follow you if they like your images. You can be the first by following one or more of their boards to set the example. Or you can wait to make sure they have enough interest to follow you and then return the compliment. All these bits of contact are opportunities to deepen the relationship. But make sure you have something in common with them to begin with.

---

6. Include your Pinterest profile link on all your social media platforms or business sites, such as eBay or Etsy. Even use this link on your e-mail signature and any physical marketing materials.

If you pursue each of these steps to drive more traffic to Pinterest, you will reap healthy rewards in the form of built-in advocates. You may have other resources as well, such as community or online organizations you're active in. Use your imagination and make it fun!

The Three Ps of Driving Traffic to Pinterest

Principle. By encouraging your existing network of clients, friends, and social media contacts to join Pinterest, you will create a network of followers and advocates. These people will pin and repin your images and ideas within their own networks and create yet more potential clients.

Practice. Check out each of the six steps above for driving traffic to Pinterest. Proactively get the word out through repeat exposure, enthusiasm, and education. Pinterest is all the buzz now; you may be the final push that people need to get involved.

Profit. The people you invite to join will become immediate followers. As they already have a level of trust with you, they will pin and repin your images to share within their own network of friends and contacts. All this action will lead to more exposure and interest in you and your product or service. This will lead to more referral traffic and sales. You gotta love it.

Spam

Lurking within all areas technical and Internet related, folks exist who just like to mess with things. While there may be no economic or social benefit to creating a virus that destroys thousands of hard drives, some people will do it anyway. Just for the kicks? Who knows? On Pinterest we don't have to worry about such severe problems. Ours is limited to the odd dose of spam.

Spam arrives in a couple of forms. First, people might repin your image of asparagus grilled with parmesan cheese with a comment like, "OMG I can't believe this really is working! I finally got the summer bod I dreamed of. Thanks to http://bit.ly/Iwe4Hq95 it's the hottest thing I have purchased all season!!!"

Now that obviously has nothing to do with grilling asparagus. But people will repin images with misleading comments in the hopes that enough viewers will click on the link and go to their website to make it worth their while.

Another form of spam is created when spammers post images with misleading links embedded in them. You click on the picture of the grilled asparagus and are taken to a suspicious website selling a "Sure Fire Way to Lose 50 Pounds in One Week!" These spammers will follow you on Pinterest hoping that you'll see you're being followed and will click on their images to learn more about who they are. Well, you'll certainly learn more about them!

At this point, spam isn't enough of a problem to worry about it. Pinterest says it's actively working on ways to identify, reduce, and eventually stop spam.

We asked Pinterest directly about spam:

Q. We write about spam in the book and Pinterest's advice and feedback on the issues (as outlined in your help forum). Is there anything further you'd like to say on that topic to reassure the user community?

A. As a growing service, Pinterest is not immune to challenges faced by sites across the web, including spam. However, it is a tremendous priority for us to quickly address them. Our engineers are actively working to manage issues as they arise. We are revisiting the nature of public feeds on the site to make it harder for fake or harmful content to get into them and have put tools in place to detect suspicious activity like automated following and commenting.

In the meantime, if you see spam, you can report it. Click on the image to bring it to full size (but not the extra click that takes you to the linked website). To the right where you can click on Like to Facebook or Tweet, you can also click on Report Pin. This opens up a menu where you can report the type of problem.

When you see any type of objectionable pin, report it. The Pinterest community is yours too, and it's up to all of us to look after it. Pinterest can then remove the image and follow that account to see if it's doing anything else less than pleasant.

Remember also that according to the Pinterest website, Pinterest doesn't do any sort of advertising, promotions, surveys, or giveaways itself on pins. If you see a pin that looks like it's doing one of these things, it's most likely spam. If you see a pin that looks too good to be true, it most likely is.

Chapter
11

Real-Time Blogger
Success Stories

*I*t's all fine and well to understand the theories of marketing successfully with Pinterest. But, as in Chapter 2, the real proof lies in
those who have actually used Pinterest to significantly boost their
business's growth. In other words, enough talk—let's see the action!

Well, in this chapter we do just that with three Pinterest superstars
who've been willing to share their success secrets and tips. You'll hear
what they're doing that's setting them apart from the crowd, and you'll
learn how to apply these techniques to your own situation. Each of these
case studies covers a blogger who uses Pinterest to increase traffic and
hence business. The fact is, what you read today might be miles out of
date from when it was written. When a business catches the Pinterest
wave, it's hard to keep up; its growth can turn exponential. But what's
important is that we learn what we can, from successful people's own
words and experiences, and apply it to our own businesses. This is exactly what we'll do here.

You'll hear from Liz Marie Galvan, who gets so many pins, repins,
e-mails, and new contacts for her business that one of her biggest challenges is simply keeping up. Courtney Slazinik has achieved such success with pinned images from her website (the most valuable kinds of

pins) that one image alone has been pinned over 16,000 times. And we'll finish with Dana Willard, whose story traverses the entire spectrum: from seeing Pinterest as a threat to her creative secrets, to embracing it such that it's now one of her top sources of referral traffic to her blog and achieving over 160,000 repins in total.

Let's get started!

Liz Marie Galvan

Liz Marie runs Lizmarieblog.com, a DIY and furniture renovating blog and classic example of turning an intangible service—DIY tips and techniques—into a thriving small business (see Figure 11.1). She also sells handmade craft items on Etsy at http://www.lizmarieshop.etsy .com. As seems to be the case with many people, she stumbled upon Pinterest by accident.

Figure 11.1 Liz Marie's pinboards aren't just DIY related. She appeals to her followers through information and images from several beauty and craft areas.

Liz Marie recalls, "My discovery of Pinterest is actually kind of funny. When I first started blogging, I would check my stats daily and see where people were coming from. I kept seeing people from this site called Pinterest. I had no idea what Pinterest was, and I clicked on it and was so confused that I never went back. Then a few weeks later one of my friends asked if I'd heard of this website called Pinterest and told me how amazing it was. I gave it another look, and once I learned how to work it, I fell in love. My life has not been the same since."

With over 3,000 followers in a short amount of time on Pinterest, Liz Marie must be doing something right. Her journey began with a growing blog whose viewers liked her content and images so much that they independently started to share them on Pinterest. This is much the same as Ben Silbermann's experience with the very first Pinterest users. Folks who understood his vision started using Pinterest without his even realizing it.

In Liz Marie's words, "I started noticing the power of Pinterest for my blog when I added the Pinterest button and it showed me how many people pinned each blog post. I was amazed when I saw the numbers in the thousands on individual posts."

What's caused this phenomenal exchange of blog posts and images from Liz Marie's site to Pinterest? (And remember, this doesn't even include the amount of repins that have surely taken place.) To begin with, she has a hip, active blog site, filled with information to make the viewers' lives better. For free, she offers techniques, advice, and before-and-after pictures to take your ho-hum garage sale furniture and turn it into something artistic and attractive. She also gives you organizing ideas for closets, jewelry, and wall space and has even been known to throw in links to her favorite tunes.

In short, she's set herself up to be an active, trusted resource for DIY ideas and shows she has great taste to go with it. Not only this, but when she discovered the amount of pinned images going to Pinterest, she quickly signed up and became an active member herself. This is the marketing circle we've emphasized before. From her blog to Pinterest and back again. And in each place Liz Marie is active and provides information, great images, ideas, and products to purchase.

Liz Marie is also cleverly working her blog site and social media platforms. She includes Like and Follow Me buttons on her site and sells advertising for an added revenue stream (see Chapter 15). Finally, when she opened her Etsy shop, she didn't just sit back and hope folks would show up; she actively informed her current followers and encouraged them to participate in her social media venues with a free giveaway. See Figure 11.2.

I wanted to kick the Grand Opening of my shop with
a little giveaway for you!!!

I am giving away $25 to my shop! That means you can get
the most expensive thing in my shop FOR FREE just enter
to win in the comments section below & I will pick one winner
next week Friday {5/11/12}

To Enter {Each one is an additional entry}:

1. "Like" Liz Marie Blog on Facebook & comment below saying you did

2. "Favorite" Liz Marie Shop on Etsy & comment below saying you did

3. Visit Liz Marie Shop & comment below your favorite item

4. "Pin" an item from Liz Marie Shop & comment below saying you did

Good luck to you all!! & again thank you for all of your support
It means so much to me.. & I'm thankful for each & every one
of you.. *sappy moment*

Ok I'm done 😊 Talk to you soon...

Liz Marie

Figure 11.2 Liz Marie campaigned to get the word out when she opened her Etsy shop.

Best Practices

Below we've listed several of Liz Marie's best practices:

- Label your pins with keywords so they can be easily found during a search.

- Label your boards with keywords and make sure to categorize them properly. Also, organize your boards so your followers are clear about what they can expect from each.

- Let your followers on other social media outlets, including your blog or website, know that you're on Pinterest and that it's a great way to stay up to date on your images and ideas.

- Add watermarks to your photos so people will always know they came from you.

- Use giveaways on your blog or website, as these bring excellent exposure.

- Use more than one form of social media and/or e-commerce site. Although new with Etsy, Liz Marie has already found that it's bringing in more e-mails, interest, and inquiries. This feeds back into both her blog and Pinterest profile and provides another revenue stream. (See Chapter 15.)

- Remember that Pinterest is a free way to market yourself. One of the most important things as a business owner is to get out there and utilize social networking. Pinterest is great for this.

> **TRAFFIC TIP**
>
> Liz Marie conducts one or two giveaways per month, and it's pretty simple. A company or shop contacts her to host the giveaway. She does a product review and asks her followers to like the company's Facebook page, tweet about the giveaway, or pin it to Pinterest, and then to leave a comment saying they did any of these. The company gets more exposure, as does Liz Marie, and her followers get the chance to win a free product. It works all around.

Liz Marie estimates her blog traffic has grown 70 to 80 percent from her Pinterest exposure. Based on the amount of comments and e-mails she receives daily saying they found her on Pinterest, she estimates her new blog followers are "in the thousands." Several of her posts have been pinned over a thousand times, and one image has been repinned over 22,000 times. (See Figure 5.1.)

Not bad for the power of Pinterest!

Courtney Slazinik

Courtney Slazinik is the owner and creator of Click It Up a Notch (http://www.clickitupanotch.com), a unique photography advice blog where you can learn to improve your photos one click at a time. She provides tips and tutorials on how to shoot in manual mode, edit, and use light-ing and composition in your photos. After her husband dropped and broke the family camera 20 minutes before she gave birth, she con-vinced him to get her a DSLR and has been hooked ever since. As a for-mer elementary school teacher and current stay-at-home mom, she has developed a passion for photography that has now become a full-blown obsession. At Click It Up a Notch, she is able to combine her love of teaching and photography in one place.

Courtney first discovered Pinterest in April 2011 when she read an article about how you can see how many of your images have been pinned on Pinterest (see "Keeping Track of Social Traffic" in Chap-ter 7). She quickly became addicted to watching her blog posts being pinned daily and reading the comments and descriptions people were leaving on the pins. She soon realized that because these pins and re-pins linked back to her blog, Pinterest could become a huge source of referral traffic.

In her words, "It wasn't until I decided to take the whole month of November 2011 off for a vacation that the impact Pinterest could have on a blog truly hit me. I didn't put up a single post from the end of Oc-tober to almost the end of November. Since I knew my numbers would drop from my lack of posting, I didn't even check my statistics. When I finally started to post again at the end of November, I checked my stats and was floored when I saw I had more hits in November than any other month when I was posting. What was my number one source of traffic? Pinterest. Not only were people finding my posts on Pinterest, but they were coming to my blog to read them as well as becoming followers. All this while I was away on vacation! Pinterest was my new best friend."

So what's Courtney's secret?

She's a natural savvy marketer. First, as with Liz Marie, her blog is full of educational advice and information—in this case on the craft and art of photography. She offers this for free and even has several other experienced photographers as monthly contributors. Her images are beautiful, and she adds personal stories and pictures so that it's easy for the viewer to feel a connection with her as an individual. She sells ad-vertising on her blog as a source of revenue.

Courtney has discovered a way to create images that are more likely to be pinned than others. "I kind of made up the phrase 'pinnable button/ image.' Not that I created the idea, but basically I use Photoshop Elements

TRAFFIC TIP

When you add the Pin It button to your blog posting, you can select the image you want pinned. Make sure you choose the most attractive image that has the best odds of being re-pinned. Use Courtney's formula below for maximum effectiveness.

to create an image that's attractive and increases its chances of being pinned, as well as putting my blog title on it. I take an image from my blog post, then add a title, my website address, and a border. Then I insert it into the top of my post and select it as my image for my Pin It button."

Figure 11.3 is a great example of an image that's more likely to be pinned. (See also Figure 9.1.) Here are the step-by-step instructions:

Figure 11.3 Courtney Slazinik's unique way of creating an extra-pinnable image. She inserts the blog title, her website, and an attractive border.

- Choose an attractive, fun photograph that fits your brand.

- Photoshop in the blog title and your website address.

- Add a border using your brand colors and style.

- Select this photo as your Pin It image.

- Insert the image at the top of your post.

Content is also a crucial factor in Courtney's success, and she tries to write something that's pinnable at least once a week. Some content is more attractive for Pinterest users than others. Although Courtney doesn't blog on all these, she's found these are the top seven most pinnable content subjects:

1. Lists

2. How-to

3. DIY

4. Recipes

5. Before and after

6. Kids' activities

7. Home ideas

We don't always think of tailoring images and content specifically for Pinterest users, but this is exactly what Courtney has done with great success. The post in Figure 11.3 was pinned over 1,000 times, and many others have been too. One blog image of hers has been posted over 16,000 times, and she figures because it's a holiday image, it'll reach new pinning highs every Christmas.

Figure 11.4 reveals several great marketing techniques in a single blog post. It's a contest, which is a great way to stimulate action and interest. It includes a call to action to enter the contest. She mentions her e-mail newsletter and allows the viewer to sign up for it right there and then: a great way to add to her e-mail list. She includes a fun pinnable image Photoshopped with her logo and website. Finally, in her comments she shows herself to be fun and human, noting that she even likes the little guy's smirk. Five different techniques in a short amount of time and space—that's something to learn from!

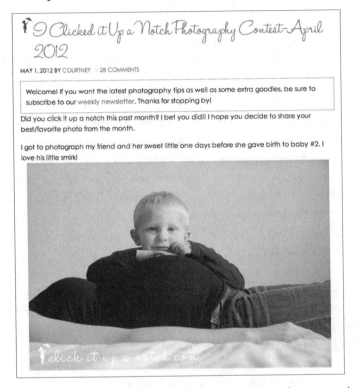

I Clicked it Up a Notch Photography Contest-April 2012

MAY 1, 2012 BY COURTNEY   28 COMMENTS

> Welcome! If you want the latest photography tips as well as some extra goodies, be sure to subscribe to our weekly newsletter. Thanks for stopping by!

Did you click it up a notch this past month? I bet you did! I hope you decide to share your best/favorite photo from the month.

I got to photograph my friend and her sweet little one days before she gave birth to baby #2. I love his little smirk!

Figure 11.4 In this one blog post, Courtney achieves several savvy marketers' marketing goals.

Best Practices

Below we've listed several of Courtney's best practices:

- Create images and content specifically with Pinterest users in mind.

- Craft your pinnable images to include your blog title and website name and add an attractive border.

- Insert Pin It buttons at the bottom of your blog posts. Choose your most pinnable image to be the one posted.

- Add your website to your profile.

- Bear in mind that taller images get somewhat more repins.

- Wherever possible, also add Facebook and Twitter buttons or those for whatever social media platforms you're using.

- Give your blog and images a brand feel. Courtney's images are often identifiable because she works with the same colors and style.

Dana Willard

Dana authors the popular DIY sewing, design, and photography blog, MADE (http://www.danamadeit.com). She's become so successful that her designs have been featured in several sewing books, print magazines, and creative websites. Recently she published her first book, *Fabrics A to Z: The Essential Guide to Choosing and Using Fabric for Sewing*, and she's working on a second book set to be published in 2013.

She discovered Pinterest like so many others, simply by hearing people talk about it and say what a cool thing it was. In her words, "In a strange way, I didn't want to join because it felt like I'd just be jumping on the bandwagon. And in another strange way, I felt threatened by the site. As a design/DIY blogger, I often shared roundup posts on my site, or I would bookmark ideas on my computer that I was inspired by, stuff that I might create my own spin on and share down the road. So I didn't want to 'show my hand' by pinning things on a board for everyone to see. I wanted them to come to my blog for that!"

Some of you might feel the same—worried that due to Pinterest's visual nature, it reveals too much of what you want to reserve for your blog or website. However, over time, Dana found the exact opposite was true. The more actively that she pinned and shared images on Pinterest and on her site, the more traffic that came to her site and to Pinterest. It's now become one of her top traffic sources. Sound familiar?

"One day I was creating a Fourth of July roundup post, and I decided to jump onto Pinterest and see what kind of images might surface. I typed 'red white blue' in the search box and was blown away by the cool photos that popped up—a huge improvement over doing a Google image search. I realized that many Pinterest users were pinning the exact things I was into: pretty pictures, yummy recipes, cool photos, and design ideas. I was hooked. It was too easy!"

For Dana, Pinterest turned from a murky threat into a priceless tool for organizing the "visual thoughts in my head." As she formed her boards, she was able to more clearly formulate her design ideas and personal style. But more important, she discovered how to make Pinterest work *for* her. She found that the more effort she put into creating interesting projects for her blog, the more likely her readers were to pin an image of those projects, and for their friends to then repin her projects, and for new people to show up at her site looking for those projects (see Figure 11.5). Pinterest is a marketing monster, working in her favor.

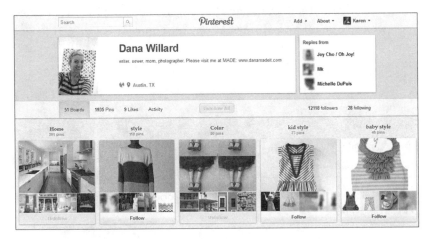

Figure 11.5 Dana Willard's Pinterest profile and a sample of her diverse array of pinboards.

Dana estimates that she now gets between 2,000 and 3,000 blog hits from Pinterest *per day*. And even when she's not posting on her blog, the referral traffic from Pinterest keeps coming in. In her words, "[Pinterest] *far* outweighs the traffic from other social media. And from my standpoint it is far more creatively interesting. I can spend an hour on Pinterest pinning away pictures, design ideas, and recipes. I love how pretty everything looks on a board. But Facebook? Eh. I'll post a link to the latest blog post and that's it. It's pretty boring (and boring looking)."

Best Practices

Below we've listed several of Dana's best practices:

- Vertical photos show up larger than horizontal ones on Pinterest. Therefore, when formatting a blog post, be sure to include a good, strong vertical image for people to pin.

- Check in with Pinterest daily (using http://pinterest.com/source/ with your website address added at the end) to see which photos are being pinned from your blog or website. This will help you understand which images captured the post visually. Learn from this, and it will help you design, photograph, and write better blog posts.

- Clearly organize your pinboards into categories of the products you share and sell. Dana adds her blog name so her followers know where to go for more information. See Figure 11.6.

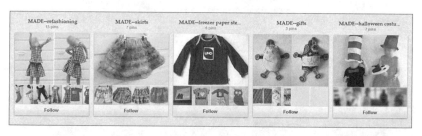

Figure 11.6 Clearly labeled and organized pinboards including the name of Dana's blog, MADE.

Dana sums up her Pinterest experience as follows, "Bottom line: instead of fighting the idea of Pinterest, I embraced it. I think of it now as a complement to my blog. It's a place for people to follow my design inspiration and styles, while my blog is where they get the DIY ideas and tutorials. I absolutely love using Pinterest, and, in a way, Pinterest uses me. I love seeing my projects pinned and repinned. It makes me happy to know that Pinterest sort of creates free marketing for my blog. By making it possible for people to pin my stuff, new visitors end up at my site. And the more visitors that come, the more advertising money I make from the ads that run on my blog. It's a win-win situation for everyone."

Part 4

PINTEREST
SELLING
STRATEGIES

Pinterest and the New Era of Social Commerce

*W*hile Pinterest began as a place to share pictures of things we love, it has quickly evolved into a premier location for social commerce. According to Wikipedia, "social commerce is the use of social network(s) in the context of e-commerce transactions." This is pretty much what we've been talking about in the last few chapters. In fact, the trend toward social commerce is so strong that Mark Zuckerberg, cofounder of Facebook, said, "If I had to guess, social commerce is the next area to really blow up."

Pinterest is a natural for social commerce and for direct selling from the site itself. One of the principal drivers of social commerce lies at the heart of the basic premise of Pinterest: discovery through people rather than search engines and bots. We've always preferred buying something or employing someone's services based on a personal recommendation. If your cubicle buddy, hairdresser, or 15-year-old daughter tells you those red Coach sneakers are pretty darn cool, you're far more likely to buy them than if you just walk past them in the store or see them online. Now take this same principle and extrapolate it to the millions of social media users the world across. The potential is staggering.

We're on the crest of the social commerce wave, and Pinterest is perfectly positioned to give you the ride of your life. The key is to understand the tools you have to work with, the environment within which you're operating, and the fundamental principles involved in encouraging people to buy your product or service.

Let's begin!

The Evolution of Buying and Selling Online

Imagine, just a few short years ago, early adopters were making their first purchases on exciting new websites called Amazon and eBay. The rest of us sat back, worried about losing our money in such a risky endeavor as *buying something online!* In those same years e-mail spread like a pandemic virus, but the good kind, where all of a sudden you could drop a note to friends, colleagues, or clients, and they received it within . . . seconds.

This world is referred to as Web 1.0, and it depicts a time when non-academics—everyday people, that is—first started exploring the vast resources online that previously were the lairs of universities and research labs.

Then came the next generation of online experiences: Web 2.0. This is where most of us dwell online today. Googling for information, like a name, recipe, or historic event, is as common as checking the yellow pages used to be. We go online to pay our bills, send Christmas cards, and, yes, buy things, all the time. We share pictures, stories, and real-time updates of our lives on Facebook. And on LinkedIn we post our résumé for all to peruse.

Amazon and eBay have grown in size and scope. They've introduced us to the first tendrils of social commerce in the form of "seller ratings" and "user recommendations." Amazon tracks your purchases and several times a week offers you new products that fit your personalized buying trends. You learn through them that people who bought *The Tipping Point* also bought *Outliers* and *Blink*. With the endless amount of data that comes streaming in from clients and browsers, you'll see that 1,280 customers reviewed *The Tipping Point* and gave it an average rating of 4.1 out of 5 stars. Crowdsourcing has reached shoppers.

Some people consider this stage, where online shopping and social media intersect, as the next generation—Web 3.0. Whatever you call it, it's the fastest-growing aspect of our online experience. And it all boils down to discovery through people.

A social media site (http://www.blippy.com) exists now where members hook up their credit card purchases to their profiles so their friends and family can see what they've just bought—in real time. On Facebook, Twitter, YouTube, and the new darling on the block, Pinterest, users are encouraged to rate posts, images, products, and ideas all the time. *Liking* and *sharing* have taken on completely new meanings from when you were sitting on the curb comparing marble collections.

It's through the recommendations of other people that more and more sales are made. What better platform for this to occur within than social media sites? It's what we're already doing; the process now is simply to streamline into sales. And Facebook has done just that with its Deal application. From Deals you have access to companies running promotional deals, and it links to your Places app so you can find these bargains within your geographic range. Statistics show when people like or share this information, sales increase dramatically.

Many more examples exist of the impact of social media on e-commerce, and they all point to a tsunami-size trend heading our way. In fact, the largest e-commerce websites in the world are benefiting from the social aspect of commerce. It's human nature for us to become advocates of something we've just purchased (see Chapter 7). We make the leap and buy something, and then we want to be validated in our decision. Getting other people excited about our new video game, or home furniture, or running shoes is one way of doing this.

Gerhard Berssenbrügge, CEO of Nestlé Germany, had this to say about social commerce and the value of consumer input on his business model:

> We want to be inspired by people's ideas and to enable them to take an active part in helping us shape not only the future of Nestlé Marketplace [Nestlé's online store], but also of our products. . . . By the end of this year, online sales of food and beverages in Germany are expected to exceed €500 million, so it is clearly an important area where we have a real opportunity to engage with customers.

When you think about it, the vast majority of our purchases are done with the influence of other people. We check user recommendations; we ask friends; we see what's cool in our social circles, on TV, and at the movies. Cultural taste affects each one of us at a surprisingly deep level. Social commerce—that is, buying and selling things based on the influence of social media—will be a major factor in our lives as consumers in the coming years.

The good news? Pinterest and your small business are positioned perfectly to take advantage of this powerful new trend. Let's look at how.

The Pinterest Edge

Because of the process of discovery through people you trust, Pinterest is at the forefront of Web 3.0. Your experience on this site and the ramifications it has for your small business match the social commerce template. Images are shared through repinning, liking, and being commented on. These statistics are displayed publicly, and the very same images can be shared via your other social media platforms.

As you build up the number of followers, you're virtually building up the number of people who will spread your ideas. They trust your opinions and will act on them. You may know some well, as in family and friends, and yet many more you'll never meet; but the trust has been established, and the avenue for social commerce is firmly in place.

The next step is to position your business to benefit from this new way of buying. In the previous chapters, we've been talking about how to increase traffic to and from Pinterest and your website and how to create the crucial emotional engagement necessary for trust to form. Now we take those factors and create direct sales from Pinterest by engaging the social commerce machine on your behalf.

The Gifts Page

The Gifts page is one of Pinterest's built-in functionalities to facilitate the direct sales process. As you learned in Chapter 5, adding a price banner is easy. Just type in the price with a dollar sign in the pin description. Pinterest will automatically create the banner on the upper left-hand corner of the image. These images then show up on the Gift feed as well as the feeds of anyone who's following you.

The advantage of the Gifts pages is that people go here specifically to shop. They're looking for a great idea within a price range. However, two issues need to be considered.

First, how do you know where you will land on the Gifts feed? As more images are posted, yours will move farther down the feed. You must post priced items regularly so that people will get used to seeing them and start following you, if they visit the Gifts feed regularly. But you must make this process—pinning priced images—a consistent marketing activity for it to work.

TRAFFIC TIP

Be careful what you write in your image descriptions when you pin or repin them. If you pin a picture of a movie star who was fined for speeding and say, "Wow, he got busted for $650!" that image will appear on the Gifts page with your name on it and a price of $650. The system can't differentiate between a random comment and a request to create a price banner!

Second, what if people aren't out shopping and don't head for the Gifts page? What if they're just cruising around Pinterest getting ideas and inspiration? You want them to see your image, know what the price is, and click on it to buy. This form of direct selling will work to augment your other marketing efforts, but you need to get people to your boards. The more repins and likes you get on any particular priced item, the more likely others will want to buy it too.

Selling Directly from Your Pinboards

This is the alternative to relying solely on the Gifts feed, and it works very well. You can organize your priced images within your normal pinboard setup. As your followers get to know you, they'll be more and more likely to buy from you.

Three distinct ways exist to organize your pinboards and priced items. Remember that each of the tools and techniques we've discussed in previous chapters regarding ways to increase traffic to your

Pinterest site will serve to increase your direct sales. It's as simple as the more people who see your priced images, the more people who will end up buying them.

1. Intersperse your priced images with your "normal" ones. This way, those who follow that board will continue to get your great content and occasionally have the opportunity to buy things too.

2. Create specific "Store" or "Product" pinboards. On these, everything is for sale, and your followers can more easily find what they're looking for. As well, this clearly delineates the purposes of the boards. For some, this is a more comfortable way to go about selling, rather than mixing it up with more personal images.

3. If you have enough salable items, consider creating a pinboard for each type. For some this is quite an effective solution. Let's say you're marketing crafts supplies and ideas. You could have a "Candle Supplies" board next to "Soap Molds and Fragrances," followed by "Easter Decorations." In this way you make it easy for your followers to find what they're looking for. Over time you will develop more followers, likes, and repins for each board; and this, in turn, will encourage prospective buyers to trust in your goods.

As always, basic selling and displaying guidelines should be followed:

- Always use excellent-quality images. These reflect back on the quality of the products and business behind them, i.e., you. Through your images, you are letting your clients know who you are.

- Place your business logo, brand, and website on all your images. This way when they get repinned, the viewer will always know exactly where they came from.

- Organize your boards in an attractive, tidy fashion. Again, your boards reflect who you are. If they're disorganized, unclear, and poorly labeled, this tells the clients you are too. If your boards are attractively displayed and organized and if the clients are easily able to work their way through them, this will tell them you're a true professional.

Seven Selling Rules

Many of the rules and maxims of selling in general apply to Pinterest specifically. In this regard, social commerce is no different from other types of commerce. Prospective clients want to like you, know you, and trust you before they'll buy from you. Consider the following guidelines that will help you achieve this, many of which will be familiar to you. The key to integrating them into your Pinterest marketing plan is to maintain a steady, active, and positive presence on Pinterest, just as we've been showing you how over the last several chapters.

1. Most buyers need to bond with you before they buy. For people to see an item and immediately purchase it is more uncommon than you might think. Rather, people know you already, have built up a degree of trust, and then are comfortable buying something you have displayed.

2. In the same vein as above, the viewer needs to be emotionally moved by the product or service itself. It must solve a problem or fulfill a passion.

3. Some products and especially some services need to be explained or demonstrated before their full value can be appreciated. This is where educational pins serve a purpose and provide the backdrop to future purchases. As you educate your followers along the way, it makes it easier for them to eventually pull the trigger and buy.

4. Buyers love testimonials and buyer feedback. This is why ratings on Netflix, eBay, and Amazon work. We trust what other people tell us more than we do the seller of the product. We've all been sold a bill of goods, but through feedback from real people we gain confidence. Testimonial pins work wonders, as do accumulated likes and repins.

5. Many people respond well to direct comparisons with competing products. This goes back to educating your clients on why your product or service is the best. You can come up with creative infographic pins to gently demonstrate your superiority.

6. A 100-percent-satisfaction guarantee will help to alleviate any remaining doubt before buyers make that final click. If it's not what they expected, they can always get their money back.

7. Many people will be spurred to make a purchase if there is an urgent need to buy your product now. This can be achieved several ways:

- Announce a limited-time offer.

- Sell items in limited quantities or editions.

- Announce a future date when your prices will go up; hence people need to buy now.

- Create a special offer that includes a bundle of items at a discounted rate.

- Offer one of your products or services for free when buyers purchase some other product or service.

Each of these seven keys will help you build the trust and rapport necessary to develop an active clientele. Consider each one and think about how you can incorporate it into your marketing strategy. Many you'll already be working on without even realizing it.

The Three Ps of Social Commerce and Pinterest

Principle. Social commerce refers to a new way of buying through social media, where products and services are recommended by other people. Pinterest is an ideal place to benefit from this new dynamic trend.

Practice. Utilize the Gifts page and set up pinboards specifically for selling your products or services. Incorporate the seven selling rules to achieve maximum effectiveness.

Profit. As you gain a trusting and active following, more and more people will be comfortable buying straight from your Pinterest image. They'll see your priced image and know already that you're a trusted resource. From there to buying your product or service is but a short click away.

Pinterest for Selling Services and Other Intangibles

urprising for some, Pinterest is actually ideal for service providers and sellers of intangibles: those that sell their ability and skill to do something for you, rather than sell a physical product. Given all the press about crafts, fashion, and home and garden DIY, Pinterest isn't the first place you think of when considering marketing your law practice, graphic design business, or plumbing services. However, some of the Pinterest users with the largest followings are similar to those.

As a provider of a service, you have every bit as much potential on Pinterest as those with physical products; you just need to adjust your approach. Marketing strategies really hit their stride in this arena. Rather than having the products themselves—your bracelets, trendy riding boots, or Lady Gaga sunglasses—do the talking for you, with intangible services you must appeal to the emotional need of the prospective client. However, this is a far more powerful avenue because you're triggering core motivators within people, not temporary whims. This can lead to long-lasting, referral-generating customers.

One of the perceived roadblocks to selling intangible products is that it's as if your clients are relying on a promise. You're virtually telling them that you promise to do something for them in the future, and based on the past this is what they can expect to happen. This is far different from boxing up your best perfumed candle and sending it in exchange for a payment. However, by understanding what the emotional drivers of your prospects are and how you can appeal to these on Pinterest through images and education, this roadblock turns into nothing more than a phantom shadow.

First let's look at real-case scenarios of successful Pinterest users within the world of services and intangibles.

Jane and Jenny and eMeals.com

Jane DeLaney and Jenny Cochran, sisters and mothers, were diehard determined to get their families eating three healthy meals a day. They started eMeals.com as a solution to their own hectic lifestyles. As they phrase it on their website, "In 2003, Jane began the task of creating a unique meal planning service that would incorporate all of the things that a mom would want to take the stress out of dinnertime. Her sister, Jenny Cochran, came alongside Jane and the two built an amazing team of meal planners who are all experienced family cooks."

While the two have gained a high degree of success through their website and other marketing endeavors (they have over 63,000 Facebook fans and have been featured by Oprah, Martha Stewart, and the *New York Times*), they're also a perfect example of selling an intangible service—weekly tailored menu plans—through Pinterest. They're using the subscription model of monetizing that we'll get into more in Chapter 15.

In a nutshell, Jane and Jenny sell subscriptions to their service. By visiting their website you can sign up for a weekly menu plan program from over 30 options. Each week they e-mail you that week's menu plan and a detailed shopping list of all the ingredients you'll need. They'll even include bargains from your favorite local stores.

Their Pinterest pinboards have images of the delicious foods you'll be serving, all of which they promise are easy to make and budget conscious, as well as boards of "Tips," "Inspiration," and the "Family Circle." In other words, they're showing you what they're delivering, and they're adding a personal touch throughout (see Figure 13.1). This helps the viewer gain trust and become emotionally engaged. All the same good stuff we've been talking about throughout this book.

Figure 13.1 eMeal's pinboards aren't just about selling services; they also include kitchen designs, ideas for kids, and specific recipe ideas like gluten-free and for the slow cooker.

Many of their images on Pinterest carry a link back to the eMeals website, where the viewer can learn more and subscribe. Other images are repins as Jane and Jenny share the good things they find on their search for healthy, budget-friendly meals. Their own images they brand with the eMeal logo, almost as if they'd read this book!

This process of sending traffic from their website to Pinterest, where their followers can share the images and ideas with their friends and followers, is a core Pinterest-savvy marketer tool. The word spreads, and more people in turn are intrigued by what they have to offer, trust is built, and traffic increases back to their website, where subscriptions are bought. The cycle feeds on itself, but no actual physical product changes hands. It's a classic example of successfully selling a service.

Maryann Rizzo

Interior design is another example of selling something on Pinterest that you can't unwrap from a package. With over 220,000 followers and counting, Maryann Rizzo certainly appears to be utilizing the Pinterest advantage for service providers. Her pinned images don't just cover living rooms and patios, but span an enormous spectrum of visually pleasing pictures. From architectural designs, to travel tips, to favorite foods, her over 290 pinboards are a feast for the eyes. Viewers can scroll through the diverse selection and follow those that appeal to their interests and passions. (See Figure 13.2.)

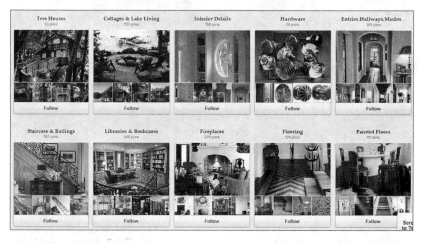

Figure 13.2 An example of the wide range of design interests Maryann Rizzo shares with her followers.

As well, her Pinterest presence clearly demonstrates a few key qualities:

- **Organization.** Each board is clearly labeled and organized. This implies she just might be organized too, a very good quality for someone in charge of how your home will end up looking.

- **Spectacular images.** This tells us she does, in fact, know what looks good. It's one thing to say you have a talent and an entirely different thing to show it.

- **Creativity.** The array of pinboards and ideas is so broad, you can't help but realize this is someone who's thinking around corners and in little-known nooks and crannies. One pinboard (with over 80 images) is devoted to nothing but tree houses. How fun is that?

- **Activity.** Maryann has pinned over 60,000 images. Most probably she didn't do this over the course of a couple of days but rather is steadily adding new content over time. This shows she's someone who's involved in life and her design work.

- **Popularity.** Okay, with over 220,000 people following her, something interesting must be going on. This statistic alone shows us the effect of social commerce in the form of people "recommending" her by following.

In short, Maryann is showing us, through her activity on Pinterest, that she's a creative, active, popular, and organized person with great taste in visual design. Interestingly, she did this entirely with pictures, not words. As the old saying goes:

A picture [or pinboard!] is worth a thousand words.

Roberta Isleib

Can Pinterest help writers? Absolutely. The concept is no different from selling any other adventure or dream. Roberta Isleib (aka Lucy Burdette) is one such example. As the author of nine mystery novels, the latest series of which stars a Key West food critic as the mystery-solver protagonist, she has an effective and intriguing Pinterest layout.

In her profile tagline she lets us know she's not only a writer but a clinical psychologist. Right away we know here's someone who might have interesting insights into human nature. Her boards then reflect the themes of her books through both murder whodunits and great food.

Roberta follows the key Pinterest-savvy marketers' tenets of educating and entertaining the viewer, not just directly via her books, but also with pinboards on Key West (where the mysteries take place), food, Key West style, the writer's life, and even a titillating board on her mystery in progress, *Fatal Reservations*. Here she lets the viewer into the inner workings of her next novel. She shares the houses she's using, the clues you might be seeing, and even a floor plan that undoubtedly will involve murder, mystery, and intrigue of all kinds. See Figure 13.3.

In Roberta's words:

At first I was simply trying to get the lay of the land [on Pinterest]—figure out which boards to choose, what to name them, and how to populate them. I knew I would want to showcase the

Figure 13.3 Mystery writer Roberta Isleib leads us on a tour of her novel in progress.

books I've written and the ones I'm in the process of writing, as well as my two "hooks," Key West and food, and my recipes. The board for the mystery I'm working on helps me visualize scenes that I will write for the book and even helps me brainstorm a bit. I hope that getting a little peek into a writer's head is fun for pinners too! (And not too scary . . .)

Fiction and nonfiction alike, whatever they write, authors can promote their work. For those who are sworn introverts, who only leave their computer and imaginary characters to walk their cats to the local cemetery, Pinterest is perfect. They can reveal their inner visions, ideas, plots, and characters through pinboards that easily attract curious readers they might never have otherwise had the chance to connect with.

As Roberta does, let people inside your novels; let them visualize your inner worlds much as you do. Educate them about writing and books, and use intriguing titles to draw people in. If you write about history, create boards with historic scenes, characters, and facts. Science is your thing? Perfect. Create boards that intrigue with far-out images, as well as educate with facts and links to more information. Use that powerful imagination and let people see how you think; then share the fact that you're on Pinterest through each of your social media plat-forms. Watch the marketing cycle begin!

The Intangible Edge

So what is it that's working with sellers of services and other intangibles on Pinterest? How can it be that with no physical product to ship, these people are still able to grow their businesses through a completely visual website?

The answer lies at the core of what drives us as human beings. Our most important decisions aren't made because we saw something cute for $9.99. We decide to buy it because we've become emotionally involved in the end result. Interior designers provide the promise of a beautiful home that reflects our own inner beauty—something we most probably don't feel is expressed enough. Jane and Jenny give the hope of organized, healthy food so that our families eat right and together.

The emotional range doesn't stop with these three examples. Lawyers provide important services when we're emotionally vulnerable. They guide us through the best solutions for those key changing points of our lives—when we are wronged, or are accused of wrongdoing, or are going through divorces, marriages, deaths, and births. None of these are taken lightly at an emotional level. Real estate brokers and financial advisors help us achieve our home style and financial goals. We're walked through the process of designing our futures.

Each of these examples shows decisions made not for a product, but for the hope and image of a better life. Herein lies the power of selling services on Pinterest. It's a natural vehicle for expressing and sharing emotions. We do this through consistency (we're trusted resources), reliability (we post appealing images regularly), shared values, positivity, and the gradual building of trust.

Five Types of Emotional Energy

In order to build trust on Pinterest, we must meet our prospective clients at an emotional level—the deeper, the better. Generally speaking, people have five types of emotional energy, which start and stop at different times for different reasons. Through Pinterest you can speak to people at each of these levels, because if your clients are moved to action through these emotional states, you can build pinboards and stories that resonate with where they are.

Let's look at each of these emotional energy states more closely and explore how you use Pinterest to communicate through each one. Remember, very few people stay in one energy state their entire lives. We may have a natural propensity for one or another, but we will shift between others in our various life stages.

Creator Energy

Otherwise known as the entrepreneurial itch. Creator energy and Pinterest are made for each other. Starting a home project, new small business, or family or just putting on a dinner party means you're searching for great new ideas. Pinterest has a community for all these niches. The odds of selling your services to creators is high because they're eager to take action; they're shopping for ideas.

Create pinboards that appeal to their sense of how-to. Teach them something new and speak to their enthusiasm via the end result. This is what's driving them. Show them what their future can look like—and show them you're the one to get them there.

Crisis Energy

These people are no less ready to buy than creators, but their motivations are the exact opposite. Crisis energy comes from people who have hit rock bottom, are in emotional crisis, and need real solutions. They may be dealing with the death of a spouse or going through a divorce, or they may have a troubled teen at home. Maybe they are about to lose their home or are struggling with their weight and health. You have an opportunity to really help these people if you position yourself as an expert and therefore a solution provider. Trust is crucial because you're dealing with difficult issues.

Several options exist for your marketing approach. Create pinboards with before-and-after shots in order to show potential clients that you understand their problem and have the solution. Use testimonial boards to give them confidence, and educate them with infographics. Speak directly to their wound and give them hope. This is the key.

Status Quo Energy

Many people exist somewhere in between creator and crisis energy. Life is cruising on an even keel, and their biggest issue might only be what to make for dinner or how to get rid of all those dandelions in the backyard. These people can be hard to sell because there's no real emotional pull. Nothing is calling to them to act now.

The best way to market to those with status quo energy is to sell them a dream. Get under their skin with something beautiful and inspirational and try to get them to take action through a radical vision. For example, if you're a landscape artist, post your most enticing images with taglines that read, "If you live in the Seattle area, I can make your yard look just like this. Call me at 555-5555."

Bored Energy

These folks are just plain bored with life. They might cruise Pinterest in the hopes of getting some sort of emotional charge, and they're not even beyond creating a negative experience just to feel excitement. Needless to say, they can be hard to sell. They're not motivated and are in a fantasy mindset. They might like the idea of living in a dream home or of having spectacular abs or physical ability, but they're too bored to actually take action.

The best you can do here is hope they see your images, follow you, and are one day inspired to take action and shift into creator energy. For many, boredom is a temporary state caused by being in a rut in life. Once shifted out of that rut—through a new job, relationship, the birth of a child, etc.—they can easily morph into a more dynamic and actionable emotional energy.

Egocentric Energy

We've all met these people—or (horrors!) been one of them ourselves. This energy occurs when people have baseless overconfidence in their own ability. No worries about remodeling the backyard or finding someone to sell their home—they know how to do it all already. However, because this belief isn't founded on facts and they're not actually experts in their project, chances are they're going to run into trouble along the way and then need your help fast and furiously. When this happens, they turn immediately into crisis or creative energy mode. It's from here you can make the sale. Egocentrics themselves won't buy because they think they don't need help. When reality comes smashing down, they turn into great buyers after all.

The only way to sell to these folks is to hope they run into you when they've shifted to a different energy: crisis or creative. It's difficult to market to them directly until they realize they actually do need help.

Business-to-Business Sales for Intangibles

So far we've been talking about your business, i.e., you selling to an individual or family—the relationship is business to consumer. However, huge opportunities exist for selling your services and intangibles to other businesses—business to business. The five different types of emotional energy still apply; however, there's a catch. At work people have different mindsets. They function and make decisions from a combination of their own personality and the culture of the company. It's not just a matter of selling to an individual. You also have to factor in where the company stands as far as your service is concerned, along with the mindset of the decision maker you're dealing with.

Fortunately, these too can be broken down into different types. Each of the four can be appealed to through proper use of Pinterest.

Explorers

These are *intrapreneurs* in corporate speak, and they are very much like the entrepreneurs of the creator emotional energy. Often these people are in sales or are in charge of developing new products or finding new markets. Your opportunity to sell these folks your service is high.

> **For most of you reading** this book, if you work at a medium-to-large company, you're probably an explorer trying to understand how to break new ground in the social media space. In this sense, our goal is to position ourselves as trusted experts to help you on your journey.

With Pinterest, the best way to position yourself is as an expert in a niche or industry. Be their go-to source for new information and ideas, and you will become their trusted resource. Educate them and provide advice in your area of expertise, and explorers will buy your services.

Guardians

These people are much like the status quo of the emotional energy states. They're not early adopters, and they're more interested in maintaining stability and protection than expanding into any new areas. Although at some stage these people must take action to keep up with the Joneses, they're not easy sells.

There is, however, one way to appeal to them through Pinterest: nostalgia, history, and preservation of the past all ring true to them. Try presenting yourself as a historian of your niche and educate them on the past.

Gardeners

These folks are in the midst of a balancing act. Perhaps it's a combination of revenue streams, products, services, and assets, but these people are meticulous in their approach to growth, just like a gardener. Gardeners will definitely use Pinterest, but you must position yourself as a flat-out master of your craft. No tricks of the trade will work here because gardeners are thorough and only go with the best.

To sell your services to gardeners, use "Testimonials" and "Portfolio of My Work" pinboards. Let viewers see what you've done and how good it is, and let them know that other people appreciate your work too. Also create boards that inspire, impress (don't be afraid to toot your horn), and show off your professionalism.

Lemmings

There's no gentle way to put it; some people are just along for the ride. They're not out to make any changes or waves; they just want their paycheck and are waiting for the weekend to roll around. Selling opportunities are low for lemmings. You need to wait until something changes in their world and they're forced into a different mindset.

One approach that sometimes works is to be a low-cost alternative. Use pinboards that speak to convenience, low price (as opposed to cheap; don't sacrifice quality), and ease and flexibility. Let them know how easily you can get the job done.

The Three Ps of Selling Services and Intangibles on Pinterest

Principle. Those selling services and intangibles have just as much potential on Pinterest as those selling physical products. However, the approach must be tailored to speak to the buyer's emotions and deep-seated needs.

Practice. Carefully consider the end result that your client is looking for. In Maryann Rizzo's case, she proves her organization and creative insight through myriad beautiful pinboards of interior design and other images. Jane and Jenny help busy mothers organize their family's meals and health. Roberta Isleib promotes mystery and intrigue. Also consider what emotional energy state your prospects might be in and if they have to work within a company culture and mindset.

Profit. As you speak to your followers' deepest emotional drivers, they will come to realize you understand them. This will lead to trust and more sales.

Incorporating eBay, Amazon, and Etsy

*M*any e-commerce platforms exist that when used in tandem with Pinterest, become leveraged beyond what they can achieve independently. eBay, Amazon, and Etsy are three such examples. Each functions fine independently, but when cross-pollinated with Pinterest, sales can increase dramatically. It all goes back to the multiplying effects of followers and fans. Whether through social media or e-commerce, the more people that are exposed to your ideas, the more that will buy.

Data show that Pinterest is already driving a significant amount of traffic to e-commerce sites, and for many people this is how they find out about Pinterest in the first place. They're actually benefiting from the rapid rise of Pinterest and its ubiquitous repinning process without even knowing about it. This effect is only magnified with the correct actions, as we'll outline in this chapter.

E-commerce platforms can be beneficially interwoven the same way as social media platforms. It's a matter of understanding the pros and cons of what you have to work from and then knowing how to leverage the various sides together so they form complements. eBay, Amazon, Etsy, and Pinterest all belong to the same broad tribe of visually based social commerce, and when used together, they can definitely enhance your small business.

The eBay Angle

If you haven't heard of eBay, then it's way past time to crawl out of that cave and join the rest of the world. With over 100 million users, eBay is one of the most active and oldest e-commerce sites in existence. Much as Amazon and Etsy, eBay provides a venue for buying and selling a wide variety of goods. However, one of the key differences with eBay is that it allows for the critical auction pricing format. Auction pricing allows for huge jumps in what you can take in for your products.

The key to intermeshing your eBay and Pinterest marketing efforts lies in the fact that they bring traffic to each other's site. Your eBay buyers will learn to find more of your items and ideas on Pinterest, and your Pinterest followers will know to click on the image and buy your product from eBay. This cycle feeds on itself, and both sites see more activity.

Although not in competition, Pinterest does have an interesting advantage over eBay in the form of the pinboard setup. Through these images and subjects, your clients get to know you as a person. And as you know, it's because of this emotional engagement that people don't just become buyers but also advocates. Pinterest will turn you from an eBay seller into a real person with values, inspiration, personality, family, and a whole lot of great taste. In this way you personalize the buying experience, and this is what turns average into spectacular.

Pinterest and eBay

Let's look at five different ways you can leverage your Pinterest experience through eBay and vice versa.

1. Post your item for sale on eBay; then pin it on Pinterest. Fortunately, eBay makes it easy to do just this. It has added the Pinterest Pin It button right alongside the Facebook and Twitter buttons. eBay knows the value of cross-pollination—the more exposure eBay sellers get, the better for the sellers and eBay. The number one rule on eBay is that the items that do best have received the most viewers.

You can also do the opposite and pin your image first on Pinterest; then post it on eBay. The key is to have the pin and the post link to each other. This way your eBay viewers can find you on Pinterest and your Pinterest followers can buy your item on eBay.

Figure 14.1 is a great example of the value of leveraging eBay and Pinterest. This is a seemingly simple wooden sign painted with a meme-like saying. After it was pinned on Pinterest, it received over 500 repins, and that doesn't count the repins of repins that inevitably occurred. The repinning happened both during and after the eBay auction, but the point remains: by pinning the eBay image onto Pinterest, the number of viewers increased substantially. These are no irrelevant numbers. Added exposure is created, and it's the number one factor in increasing eBay sales and prices.

2. Add your eBay user name and any other important details to the description of the pin or the image itself. Make it as easy as possible for people to find you, follow, and buy. eBay listings are only available for 90 days after the end of the auction, and so by adding your user name, people can still hunt you down for more great stuff.

3. eBay allows you to add a link on your item listing to a photo-sharing site. At this time, Pinterest qualifies. So create a Pinterest pinboard with additional images of your auction item and then add this link to your item on eBay. As well, add the Follow Me On Pinterest button. The pinboard link will take your viewers to the specific pinboard, and the button will take them to your profile. Both these avenues will create interest and more followers.

4. Mention your Pinterest profile and add a Follow Me On Pinterest button to your eBay About Me page. The more you get the news out about where you can be found, the more people will end up following you. Sometimes they won't necessarily buy the specific eBay item they discovered you from, but after clicking on your Pinterest profile, they'll see that you have a plethora of other great ideas and products. This can help convert onetime auction viewers into long-term Pinterest followers.

5. In the eBay item description of your product, ask viewers to share the image to Pinterest. This is done by clicking on the Pinterest

Figure 14.1 This wooden sign by Kathy Wood Wooden for sale on eBay received over 500 repins on Pinterest.

Figure 14.2 Ask viewers to share your item on Pinterest by clicking on the Pinterest icon in the bottom right-hand corner.

sharing icon, like the ones you see for Facebook and Twitter. See the bottom right-hand corner of Figure 14.2.

The Three Ps of Pinterest and eBay

Principle. Encouraging your eBay buyers to visit you on Pinterest, and your Pinterest followers to check out your eBay profile, will increase qualified traffic to both sites.

Practice. Incorporate the five steps above to make it easy for your viewers to visit you on either site. This entails telling them and adding links and Follow Me On Pinterest buttons. Don't be shy; get the word out.

Profit. Your eBay buyers will be inspired by all the other great things they see on your Pinterest pinboards. This will allow them to emotionally bond with your message and brand in a deeper way. Your Pinterest followers will know to go straight to eBay to buy your product in a safe and effective environment. This cycle creates more exposure and trust, which both lead to more sales.

Pinterest and Amazon

Amazon provides a somewhat different experience integrating with Pinterest, but still, opportunities exist. The issue is that there are two ways to sell on Amazon.

First, you can become an Amazon seller. At the most basic level, you either send the physical product to your buyers yourself or outsource the shipping. Through Fulfillment By Amazon you can ship your products to Amazon, and it will sell them and send them out for you. You can also set up your own website "storefront," which Amazon supports.

Or you can become an Amazon Associate through the company's affiliate program. Amazon makes affiliate marketing easy. You earn fees by advertising Amazon products on your network, website, or blog. Each time a viewer clicks on the product icon from your site and makes a purchase, you get paid. However, Pinterest forbids the use of affiliate marketing on its website and is actively removing affiliate links from pins.

So what should we do as Amazon sellers on Pinterest? Let's look at six easy steps:

1. Include Pinterest share icons and Follow Me On Pinterest buttons on your Amazon seller website and on the description page of each item. Make it easy for your Amazon viewers to visit you on Pinterest.

2. Pin images from your Amazon site onto Pinterest so that the link remains intact. You can also do the reverse and post Pinterest images on your Amazon site. Either way, you get the cycle going back and forth, as with eBay.

3. Categorize the products you're selling on Amazon into organized Pinterest pinboards. Clearly title them and add taglines.

4. Choose to paint with a broad brush or a detailed one. In other words, do you want your boards to display every single item you hope to sell? Or would you rather have a best-of-the-best approach and isolate your finest images and products on one or two boards. Both work, but think about which way suits your business and personality the best.

5. Add additional boards that answer questions, educate, and inspire your viewers.

6. In both your Pinterest and Amazon profiles, mention that you can be found on either. Provide links for your viewers.

The Three Ps of Pinterest and Amazon

Principle. The same principle exists here as with eBay: the more traffic you get moving between the sites, the better your exposure and ability to bond emotionally with your clients.

Practice. Incorporate the above six steps into your Amazon seller business model. Together these will facilitate increased traffic between the two sites.

Profit. No surprise here—as exposure and trust increase, so do sales. It's almost starting to sound easy!

Pinterest and Etsy

While Etsy is somewhat less known than eBay and Amazon, it still packs a powerful e-commerce punch. Approximately 39 million unique visitors log in to Etsy every month, and $340 million was made in sales in 2010. At one level Etsy behaves much like eBay. You list an item for sale with a price, someone buys it, and you ship it to the buyer. Simple. But differences abound. For one, whereas you can buy or sell most anything on eBay—from household goods, to cars and airplanes, to the claimed bottled spirits of ancestors—the spectrum of products on Etsy is limited. They must be handmade by you or must be vintage (defined as more than 20 years old), or they can be crafts supplies. In the website's words, "Etsy is the world's handmade marketplace."

Whereas on eBay interested buyers bid for your product in an online auction, buyers on Etsy have only one price, the one you set, to choose from. The formula seems to be working. About 14 million registered users have set up over 800,000 "shops," the Etsy term for seller accounts. Over 13 million items are available on an average day, and a whopping 1.4 billion page views occur every month.

Although sales are in the hundreds of millions every year, fewer than 1,000 sellers make over $30,000, and just a handful make over $100,000. On the other end of the scale, many sellers make only pennies per hour, and that's no way to run a business.

Let's look at the Etsy situation in more detail.

Etsy Pros and Cons in Relation to Pinterest

Etsy has a wonderful set of benefits for craft and vintage goods small-business owners. The overall setup puts buyers and sellers together within a unique market.

- The number one benefit of Etsy for sellers is that it drives traffic to your business. This is done through the direct purchase of your item from the Etsy site.

- Buying and selling on Etsy is easy and safe.

- You can create a community of buyers by belonging to Etsy circles.

- When you list an item, you can see how many times it's been viewed, and people can "favorite" your item to come back to it later.

- People can like and share your goods through Facebook, Twitter, and, of course, Pinterest.

- When one of your items is pinned from Etsy to Pinterest, an attribution link is placed on the pin indicating your Etsy store name and providing a clickable link to your store. That allows people to find you as an Etsy seller, even if that individual item may have been removed from your store.

- With Etsy you are plugged into the social media and social commerce venues. As you learned in Chapter 12, this is key to staying on top of new e-commerce trends.

- Etsy is one of the primary destinations of Pinterest browsers.

So at first blush, Etsy is a great way to sell your products online, while taking advantage of the relationships created through social media. But let's also look at some of the other issues that have come up with Etsy as it's grown and matured.

- The goods you sell are limited to handmade or vintage items. Eventually, many people want to branch out into other areas, and the momentum developed on Etsy will be useless for those creations.

- Etsy doesn't allow auction selling. As a start-up business, auctions are the single best way to significantly increase your prices.

- Copycats are alive and thriving on Etsy. If something of yours sells well, copycats can quickly replicate your work and compete with you on price. The Etsy system will list these right next to your own goods, which guarantees price wars and disloyal clients. You can't blame your clients; of course they want a better deal. But the goodwill you're building is quickly undermined by this aspect of the system.

- Etsy's "do not contact after purchase" policy means just that—you can't contact customers after they purchase your product. This makes it difficult to nurture those critical relationships and grow your customer base. One way around this is to put a personal thank-you note in each package you send. In your note, you can include your contact details, but it would be more streamlined if the system itself allowed contact.

- The social commerce angle is reduced by not allowing contact after purchases. In order to take advantage of this crucial trend, you must be able to check in with clients. This layer of attention increases the likelihood they'll like and share your goods with their social networks. It's a shame because this in turn would bring more business back to Etsy.

- Etsy (and eBay) creates a platform-as-provider effect. This means it's Etsy's brand and customer loyalty that's being built, not yours. When your buyers look back at their purchase of your beautiful handmade soap, they'll remember they bought it on Etsy, not necessarily from you. From a savvy marketer's perspective, this is definitely the wrong response. You want your brand to be what they associate their purchase with, so they can come right back and purchase more with their friends in tow. If they say, "I need some more handmade soap so I'll hop on Etsy and buy it," you've just lost out. Etsy has won.

- Your product doesn't link directly back to your website. This makes it harder to get your full set of social media networks involved, and it makes it harder to get your brand recognized over Etsy's. It keeps the traffic at Etsy.

The Pinterest-Etsy Combination

Pinterest and Etsy, when done right, work together to leverage your overall experience. With the proper actions, you can get a circle of traffic going from Etsy to Pinterest and back, and to your other social media networks as well. You'll get more visitors to Etsy to buy your goods, and you'll get more followers on Pinterest who like your products.

Below are five steps to benefit from the Etsy-Pinterest combination:

1. When you list items on Etsy, pin them also on Pinterest. The Pinterest Pin It button is automatically included on Etsy. This gets you double exposure. It also allows more viewers to go straight to your Etsy profile because that's where the link will take them.

2. Create and organize Pinterest pinboards to attractively and logically display your Etsy products using keywords. If scarves are your thing, try *Red Scarf Board, Silk Scarf Board, Cashmere Scarves,* etc. This will facilitate the smooth flow of buyers between Pinterest and Etsy.

3. Proactively make sure your Etsy user name is displayed on Pinterest. Do this in your Profile page tagline and in the description of your pins. You can also place your Etsy user name on your images

with Photoshop. Your followers will see that you're active on Etsy and visit you there.

4. When your images are repinned, comment on them. Thank the person for repinning them and include your Etsy user name. This helps facilitate the social commerce angle. The more emotional connections you make with people, the more likely they are to follow you and eventually purchase your goods.

5. Integrate your other social media outlets with Pinterest and your Etsy-branded images. Share them to Twitter and Facebook and include them in your e-mail newsletter. Again, just getting your name out there is half the battle. Use every avenue you have to share the wonderful things you have for sale.

The Three Ps of Pinterest and Etsy

Principle. Etsy is a productive marketplace for handcrafted and vintage goods, but yet has limitations that Pinterest can help you overcome. When you integrate your traffic between these sites, exposure and sales will increase.

Practice. Use the five steps above to help Etsy and Pinterest traffic feed off each other. Pin your Etsy images on Pinterest and include your Etsy shop name whenever possible. Share these images with the rest of your social media networks.

Profit. Using the Pinterest platform to advertise your Etsy products will bring more buyers straight back to Etsy and you. It's easy to be active in both these communities because so much of what they do overlaps. This increased traffic means more sales, yet again!

Monetization Strategies for Pinterest

*G*athering more and more traffic to Pinterest and your website is all good and well, but if you don't have solid ways to turn this flow of prospects into sales, then for a small-business owner all that work has been for naught. The bottom line in marketing means increasing the bottom line. Therefore, this chapter is all about converting traffic into money. If it were easy, there wouldn't be a need for books to be written about it. We all would be rich and happily counting the dollars in our accounts. However, proven techniques exist to give you the best opportunities possible, and Pinterest is a great way to enhance these techniques.

Every business is different, and yours will certainly be unique, but most can benefit from a second or third stream of revenue. This is part of the magic. Creating a robust monetization model isn't just about increasing your primary source of revenue, although that's certainly important. It's also about diversifying the sources of revenue so you can withstand a drought in one area while you enjoy the harvest in another. The goal is to reduce risk while increasing revenue; the good news is it's possible.

Along with creating multiple sources of revenue, it's vital to clearly understand which monetization strategies are working and which aren't. In this regard, tracking your progress is critical. To simply say "Gosh I made more this month" isn't enough. You need to be able to say "Strategy A increased by 14 percent, B by 57 percent, and C left us hanging with a –3 percent." Only in this way will you be able to adjust, focus, and optimize your Pinterest monetization strategies.

Monetization Basics

When we speak of monetization, we mean ways of creating revenue from your business. The best strategies mean multiple sources of sales, repeat sales, and upselling current clients into bigger and better products or services. Your unique and personal business will morph from a trickling stream into a wide and flowing river of happy, referral-generating clients. While we'll be talking for awhile about general website revenue, remember the role that Pinterest plays is a crucial part in generating traffic that leads to sales. The Pinterest marketing efforts we've been discussing need to be in place so that you're generating traffic in the first place.

Websites that have highly evolved monetization strategies have the following four high-value benefits:

1. They make more money with fewer visitors. Each client and prospect is qualified, and several opportunities exist for people to buy.

2. With multiple sources of revenue, risk is lowered.

3. Income stabilizes. Rather than having one big month followed by a dry spell, your revenue is steady and grows at a consistent rate.

4. Customers are generally treated better because their individual value is higher.

One issue that continually comes up is how to sustain the impact of your strategy: You may begin with a successful strategy, but over time its influence fades. Customers become weary of the tactics and go elsewhere. With quality strategies this will happen far less often. Your methods of generating revenue become part of your brand and business persona.

The Four Product Revenue Structures

At the most basic level, only four combinations exist for the typical small-business owner in regard to what kind of product he or she sells and from where:

1. **Selling your own product or service from your own website.** You own IncredibleWidgets.com, and from here you sell the widgets you made yourself.

2. **Selling your own product on someone else's website.** You sell your incredible widgets on eBay, Etsy, or a similar site.

3. **Selling someone else's products on your site.** IncredibleWidgets .com markets widgets from all over the world.

4. **Selling someone else's products from someone else's site.** You sell other people's widgets on eBay, Etsy, or a similar site.

It's not rocket science; it's just a view of the basic structure from which we'll be working. Any of the four structures above works well for making money. You can begin with one, the one that your business most naturally fits, and then expand into others. In doing so, you create a more robust monetization system to strengthen your overall flow of money.

Measure, Monitor, Manage

Before we get tucked into the main course, it's crucial to understand the value of keeping track of the results you get from your revenue strategies. If you don't measure your progress, you won't know what to change. You're shooting yourself in the foot with the start gun.

First, clearly record what your revenue is now on a weekly, monthly, and annual basis. Next, make sure you know, to the best of your ability, where it's coming from. For example, let's say you sell homemade candles and soaps from your website:

- How many candles versus soaps do you sell?

- Which types sell the most? List them in order of most sales to least.

- Where does your website traffic come from? Sign up for Google Analytics and install the tracking ID on your website if you don't have it already.

- How many site visits does each social media site generate?

- How many pins and links are there from your website back to each social media platform? (In other words, where are people coming from, and where are they going with your images?)

- Can you determine which traffic referrals are generating sales? Is one source of referrals more likely to buy than another?

- Take your total monthly revenue and divide it by the total number of website visits you had in that same month. This will give you a dollar value per visit. Watch this number change; it's fascinating.

- For each new revenue strategy that you incorporate, keep the same detailed set of numbers. Total them to give your company's progress as a whole.

Recalculate these statistics at least monthly. If you can spare the time, do them weekly. Only in this way will you have a clear baseline to work from and ongoing numbers to watch as your business grows. By isolating the results from each avenue, you'll be able to see what's working and what's not. Record any adjustments you made and the date. By measuring, monitoring, and managing, you take control of your revenue flow—a very good thing to do.

Selling Your Products from Your Website

Let's begin with the most basic structure and one that many of you will be working from or began with. Fortunately, several ways exist to increase revenue.

The setup for selling objects from your website is simple. Create your products; then post images of them on your website along with posts to inspire and educate. Share these images and posts to Pinterest and your other social media outlets. Use the marketing strategies outlined in this book to increase traffic and, therefore, revenue. This method is cheap and straightforward and gives you enormous control over how your products are presented to prospective clients.

The issues are twofold. First, it takes time and effort to build up enough traffic to start bringing in significant revenue. Second, pricing is a tricky thing to master. Price your items too low, and you leave money on the table. Price your items too high, and no one will buy, but you won't be able to determine if that nonbuying is because of the high price or other reasons, such as the perceived quality of the item, the product description, or the general appeal of the item. One way around this dilemma for a new business is to use auctions on eBay to determine the interest level and customer support for your item. You'll quickly learn the pricing constraints of your product, and then you can take those lessons to your website selling efforts.

Mass-Producing Your Products

One option for making more money is to increase the quantity of goods you sell on your website. At this point, however, you run into the only-so-many-hours-in-a-day issue. However, many companies exist that will mass-produce your products based on a prototype with your specifications. If you can buy this product from them and mass-sell it on your website for a profit, then you have a viable business model.

Yet another option is to work with a company that supplies products that fit your niche. You hire these people to brand their products with your logo and then you sell them from your website. One such company is the Bella Company (http://www.bella.com). Again, if the numbers work, you may have something worth considering.

A downside to mass-producing your products is that you're still in charge of fulfilling the orders and handling the customers. However, if you can find a way to outsource this too for a decent price, you may be onto something interesting.

Selling Your Products on a Third-Party Platform

This strategy can be used as a primary source of revenue or as an adjunct to selling your products from your own website. Doing the latter gives you two separate streams of income. The primary third-party selling platforms are eBay, Etsy, Amazon, and Craigslist. However, others exist, and you might find one that caters to your particular need. For example, Dollabee.com is a site created to help doll-related sales. See Figure 15.1.

Figure 15.1 Check for niche third-party selling platforms that might fit your business, like dollabee.com does for doll makers.

Use the marketing strategies explained in this book to increase the flow of traffic among Pinterest, your website, and your third-party platform. If you have an Etsy account, for example, be sure and announce your presence on each different site. Pin images to Pinterest and let people know of your Etsy business in your pin description. If you're using eBay, you have the fabulous opportunity to up your price points through auction sales.

But most important, selling your products on a third-party platform gives you another stream of revenue to complement sales from your website. The two can feed off each other.

Selling Information Products

Information is one of the hottest products going. People will pay regularly and at high prices for the ability to learn something. For a small-business owner on Pinterest, the sale of something as intangible as information carries the opportunity for multiple streams of revenue. You can sell your own or other people's information products in the form of CDs, videos, a series of online classes, e-books, newsletters, white papers, etc.

If you sell your own information, you have the advantage of being perceived as the go-to expert. Market this, emphasizing your unique strengths and what you bring to the table that isn't available anywhere else. In this way you increase value and reduce competition. Clearly explain what advantages your followers can expect to gain from you. People will come to you and buy what you have to teach them because they can't get it anywhere else.

Marketing Information Products Through Pinterest

This is easily done by creating pinboards specific to your message:

- Create a board explaining what the problem is: having trouble losing weight, not sure how to go about writing that novel, unable to deal with a troubled teen living at home.

- Create a board explaining your expertise. Include whatever applies to prove your credentials: infographics on your education and career, testimonials, images and links to other sources of information that show you know your stuff.

- Create a board explaining how you have the solution. Here's where you market your actual information product in whatever form of packaging it might take. For example, the viewers learn you have a great new weight loss program, and they understand you have the expertise to deliver on this. Maybe you're full of great ways to market your small business on Pinterest (http://www.PinterestPower .com!), or your extensive training and practice in child psychology makes your 10-Step Program to Help Troubled Teens credible.

- Finally, create a board showing your followers what the world looks like when their problem has been solved. This is the second leg of the driving motivators for the purchase in the first place: you start with the problem and end with the solution. In the middle you explain why you're the best person to do the job.

As with all your Pinterest campaigns, make sure your images are incredible, link them properly to your website, redistribute the images and information to all your social media outlets, and be an active participant in your social media communities.

Additional benefits to selling information products include:

- They don't take up shelf space, literally.

- They're easy and cheap to replicate. Once the video or e-book is made, you just send it out to clients. CDs are a low-cost alternative if you want to send out an actual physical product.

- Premium price points can be set. Physical products (books included) sell within a fixed price range. However, digital information can be given away for free or sold for thousands of dollars per virtual package. The better you position yourself as the expert with a valuable and unique solution to your clients' problem, the higher your price can be.

- If you don't have unique information to provide, sell other people's information products. Set yourself up as a source of knowledge in your niche and offer several different information packages.

Adding Revenue Streams

Now that you have your information products and know how to market them, several options exist for where sales are actually made. Use one or all of these—whatever suits your circumstances:

- **From your own website.** This is a no-brainer and melds with Pinterest marketing perfectly.

- **From a third-party platform.** As above, easy.

- **Via your e-mail marketing campaigns.** This works especially well when intertwined with at least one of the above two options.

- **From Pinterest directly.** To do this, install a one-click shopping cart URL link to your product. When viewers click on your image, they are taken directly to the shopping cart. Make sure you include a call to action in your description, such as "Get started today. Click here to purchase!" Check out http://www.oronjo.com for shopping cart technology.

Selling Services

Many of the techniques involved in selling services are the same as for selling information. When you think about it, they're really the same thing. You provide a service based on the knowledge and expertise you have and your client doesn't. The actual products, however, are a bit different: in the former you sell a service you provide, and in the latter you sell information so that buyers can take action themselves. For example, are you offering to invest people's money for them, or are you providing them with information through a newsletter so that they can do it for themselves?

Let's say that in the selling services arena you're a landscape gardening expert and want to sell that service as a consultant. Or, your niche as a personal trainer may have a need for coaches and mentors and you can position yourself as such. If public speaking on your topic is your thing, market this skill. Perhaps you're a ghostwriter, website builder, or graphic artist. All these can easily be marketed and turned into revenue streams by following the same steps as in selling information.

Selling Subscriptions and Continuity Products

Charging for access to your website or for a regular e-mail newsletter can be a great way to set up recurring income. The key is that you must have information no one else does and that you present yourself as a true industry or niche leader. Once your prospective clients see you as the expert in fulfilling their need on a long-term basis, they'll have no problem paying for the latest and best information.

In pricing, you have a full range of choices. You can charge a lot and have a restricted and highly qualified clientele. Or you can charge less and aim for a high quantity of subscribers. For example, receiving $9.99 a month from 1,000 subscribers adds up nicely.

Selling Advertising

This strategy works well if you already have a fair amount of traffic flowing to your website. You simply allow other folks to place ads along the top in banner form or down either side (see the blogger examples in Chapter 11).

One option for selling advertising is to use the leader in this category, Google Adsense. It's easy to implement, and you can begin earning a small amount of money per click immediately. Another option is to sell advertising space yourself. This can be more profitable, but you have the additional work of administering the program yourself. Definitely look into services that automate the process.

Sell Your Website or Business

If you're a builder, not a manager, this may be the route for you. Once you've built up your traffic and clientele and structured a robust monetization formula, you have in essence created a moneymaking machine. This most certainly has value, and a marketplace exists for just such situations. Check out http://flippa.com. It's the largest site dedicated to buying and selling websites.

Case Study

Let's take all this theory and put it into practice with an example. We'll start with selling a homemade product from your website and see how many additional ways to make money we can introduce. We'll count the total number of revenue streams next to each monetization strategy added.

For our case study, assume that you are an expert wood turner. You make fabulous wooden bowls for special occasions and for decoration. You sell your products on your own website (revenue stream 1). In an effort to up your price points through auction pricing, you decide to open an account on eBay and market your bowls (revenue stream 2).

Next, you round up your wood-turning friends and offer to sell their products on your website for a commission (revenue stream 3). As your eBay reputation builds, you offer to sell your friends' products there too (revenue stream 4).

Your Pinterest Power marketing strategies are kicking in, and you're seeing new highs in referral traffic each month. Based on e-mails you receive from website visitors, you realize there's a demand for teaching people how to make beautiful hand-turned bowls like yours. So you decide to create a *Wood Turning Tips 101* video for sale on your website and eBay (revenue streams 5 and 6). You also decide to set up a direct URL link on your best Pinterest images so that your followers can purchase your video directly (revenue stream 7).

Next, you decide an opportunity exists for one-on-one online teaching of bowl-turning techniques and feedback. You and your students can chat live through Skype and exchange images and videos of the wood-turning lessons' results. You sell this service through your website (revenue stream 8).

By this time you've built up quite a reputable e-mail address list. You market your bowls directly to these people (revenue stream 9). To top off your revenue streams, you begin selling your bowls on Etsy and Craigslist too (revenue streams 10 and 11).

That's a whopping total of 11 revenue streams for your one passion: wood turning. Now that's the magic of monetizing effectively.

The Three Ps of Monetization Strategies

Principle. A precise and logical approach to creating multiple streams of revenue from your business will make you more money. Most businesses provide the opportunity for more than one way to monetize.

Practice. Choose from the above list of monetization strategies and select those that suit your business and personality. Record in detail how much your current revenue is and where it is coming from. Then update this information at least once a month and isolate income from each revenue strategy. Monitor the results and make adjustments according to what's working best and what's underperforming. Give each new strategy some time to take effect.

Profit. The more sources of revenue coming in, the more money you'll make. As well, if one source dries up, you have others to keep the money river flowing.

Marketing Campaigns for Pinterest

*T*argeted marketing campaigns are a way to bring together all the tools and techniques you've been learning so far about how to grow your small business with Pinterest. These are big-picture projects that can last months or years. Used properly, they can alter the landscape of your business and truly shift it to a new level.

It's important to distinguish between campaigns and tactics. Tactics are smaller activities and projects that can be used independently or can be implemented to support campaigns. Examples might be utilizing Pinterest price banners or creating the habit of asking folks who repin your images to follow you. These are all great actions and will help your overall marketing results. The difference with a campaign is that it entails a much bigger picture. Rather than isolated actions, a campaign is a broad vision that will dramatically impact sales. Of course, it also requires more work and discipline.

Long-term goals for your company will include the three primary business drivers: finding new clients, encouraging current clients to purchase more or again, and upselling people to a higher level of buying. Campaigns can include any or all of these big-picture goals, and Pinterest provides an excellent venue. You'll notice that many of the actions and ideas we mention overlap with what you've previously read. This is natural and a very good thing in that tactics and techniques pay benefits in myriad ways.

The most important marketing campaign you should be involved in is capturing the names and e-mail addresses of your clients and prospects. In fact, this is the most important marketing activity you can do online. E-mail is still the most direct and useful way to contact people, and that's not going to change for a very long while. We'll spend most of our time in this chapter on this strategy. However, before we dive in deep, two additional strategies exist that can be of enormous help.

Nurture Campaigns

Once you have new prospects, you need to build trust and rapport with them in order to gain a deeper level of engagement and commitment. They may have yet to purchase your product or service, or they may have purchased and you want to express your thanks and develop a deeper relationship.

Try these approaches:

- Use e-mail campaigns (see later in this chapter).

- Offer something for free: a consultation, small gift, or other small token that will provide a sample of your services.

- Send thank-you cards. Your mom was right, always say thank you, and a card provides a wonderful personal touch.

- When you find an online coupon, pin the image onto your pinboards, or even create one titled "Bargains I Found." Your clients will appreciate the effort you've made to save them some money.

- Use some of the Pinterest social engagement tactics we've discussed before—for example, following your clients (the highest Pinterest accolade), repinning and liking their images, and making positive comments.

Sales Campaigns

The primary goal here is to extend an offer so good that the client jumps in and buys. Through the act of creating a great bargain, you're helping the client take that final step.

Try these approaches:

- Create your own coupon, post it on your website, and then pin the image onto Pinterest. See Figure 16.1.

- Use a promotional price available only on Pinterest. Create a pin that shows this and the product; then pin it from your website.

- Run special-event sales, like the Fourth of July or holiday specials. Again, clearly state what the bargain is and for how long it will be available—"50% Off Until January 1st!"—and Photoshop it onto your image. Then pin this image from your website.

Great coupon!

Figure 16.1 Coupons are an effective way to offer a repinnable bargain.

The Three Ps of Nurture and Sales Campaigns

Principle. Incorporating nurture and sales campaigns will help you develop new clients, develop repeat sales, and scale up what they're buying.

Practice. Use whichever tactics above suit your specific situation. Measure the results and repeat those campaigns that provide the best returns.

Profit. By actively engaging your prospects and clients, you provide various opportunities for them to buy. Everybody loves special attention and a bargain. The techniques above will encourage more people to click the Buy button.

E-mail Marketing Campaigns

As we mentioned earlier, e-mail marketing is the single most important campaign you can incorporate to increase sales. It lies at the heart and soul of online marketing. Several reasons exist for this. First, you need a way to go to the clients, rather than wait for them to show up and buy something. E-mail gives you a way to proactively be in touch and let them know the wonderful things you have to offer.

Second, online platforms come and go. A few years ago MySpace was all the rage; now it's Facebook. In the next few years? It doesn't matter what the hot platform is if you have your clients' and prospects' e-mail addresses. Whatever venue you're working from, you'll be able to get in touch with them. As well, let's say you've been selling your items on eBay and want to give Etsy a try. Just shoot out an e-mail to the people on your list to let them all know of the change. Without this tool it would be difficult indeed to spread the word.

Finally, and most important, e-mail lists themselves are a great way to make sales and, therefore, money. This is really the gut of the beast. Send out a special offer via e-mail and sit back and watch the "Notifications from Paypal" start chiming in as people participate in your offer. You must time this carefully and not overuse or abuse your e-mail strategies, but when done properly, they're a license to print money.

Myth Busting

A couple of myths circulate the online ether like childhood ghost stories that still cause you to check under the bed at night. Let's dispel them right from the start:

- E-mail is not dead. In fact, it's alive and well and growing. Social media has built in e-mail-like functions, but e-mail is still the primary method of communicating via the Internet.

- People really do want to receive your e-mails. If you've qualified the people on your contact list and collected their e-mail addresses in a professional and legitimate manner, then the people are there because they want to hear from you. Don't think you're being a pain when you send out e-mails; rather, you're providing a wanted service.

Managing Your E-mail List

Before we go any further, it's crucial you choose a professional e-mail management system. What's this mean? Because you may end up with tens of thousands of names and addresses, you'll need an efficient way to manage your list as it grows. Outlook, Gmail, and Yahoo! just aren't designed for this. Fortunately, other companies have stepped in to fill this niche.

The three most popular services are Aweber, Constant Contact, and MailChimp. All work well, and most of the time you can get started for free. After your list reaches a certain size, you'll be required to upgrade to a paying service. Check out these services and any others that have been recommended to you. Then choose the one that fits best and start gathering e-mail addresses!

Building Your E-mail List

You can approach building your e-mail list as a series of best practices, or you can do it through the pursuit of outright e-mail or lead-generation campaigns. Both work. It's a matter of focusing certain marketing endeavors to include the simple goal of capturing the prospective customers' names and e-mail addresses.

Most marketers draw a distinction between a social media fan, or follower, or subscriber, and a true "lead." While this line is blurring within social commerce, it still holds relevance. So sometimes you'll hear e-mail campaigns referred to as *lead-generation campaigns*.

An excellent way to ask for e-mail addresses is in exchange for something of value. Let's look at the following six examples. Some you will be able to execute through Pinterest, while others can be carried out through your website.

1. **Ask viewers to provide an e-mail address in exchange for viewing content on your website.** Although considered an aggressive option,

many marketers are using this technique with significant success. You install a pop-up window that doesn't allow the viewers access to your website content until they fill in their name and e-mail address. This is considered "interruption marketing," which some people consider distasteful. The choice is yours. See Chapter 19 for more information on how to add an e-mail-collection pop-over window.

2. **Offer a free newsletter.** This is a common method and serves the dual purpose of getting new e-mail addresses and also qualifying your contacts in that they most definitely want to hear from you again. See ideas for what to include in your newsletter below. You can do this on your website and Pinterest.

TRAFFIC TIP

One option is to sign people up for your newsletter directly from Pinterest. This way there's no need for them to go to your website first. Create a pin detailing the advantages to subscribing to your free newsletter. Then click on Edit and paste the URL to either your e-mail management system or your landing page. Now, when the viewers click on the pin image, they'll immediately be able to sign up.

3. **Offer something else for free.** Offer an e-book, report, white paper, or whatever else might be relevant for your niche. Again, this strategy can be applied to your website and Pinterest pinboards.

4. **Hold contests.** We looked at myriad advantages of contests in Chapter 9; however, contests can also be used in the context here. To gather e-mail addresses you add the additional step of creating a contest landing page. This page only exists for the duration of the contest and is designed for one purpose: to gather contact information, as shown in Figure 16.2. Once the viewers fill in the form, they can participate in the contest. See Chapter 19 to learn how to create lead capture landing pages.

Figure 16.2 A classic landing page used by Aqua Hotels and Resorts for its Pinterest contest.

5. **Offer webinars and special online events.** Create an educational webinar or other online event where viewers must use their name and e-mail address to sign up. For more information on creating a webinar, see Chapter 19. Promote the event on your website and pin this image onto Pinterest. Like and comment to those that re-pin your image.

> **In Jason's experience:** I created a *10-Part Marketing on Pinterest Bootcamp* video series where the only price of entry for viewers was to sign up with their names and e-mail addresses. I promoted it with my regular followers on Pinterest and ended up with over 250 new names and e-mail addresses in the first few weeks. Then as this book was made available on Amazon for presale, I e-mailed them the details and asked them to consider "paying me back" by preordering the book.

6. **Use paid advertising.** As of this writing, Pinterest doesn't support a paid advertising system like Google Adwords. However, as several of Ben Silbermann's roots extend into this turf from his time working for Google, some people believe Pinterest will support some type of paid advertising system in the future. Keep your eyes out for this ability on Pinterest and think about how you can tie it into gathering e-mail addresses.

E-mail Marketing and Pinterest

The variety of objectives for which you can use your e-mail list is limited only by your imagination. The key is that you are now in control of when contact with your clients and prospects is made. You can go to them with your information, ideas, and irresistible bargains.

First of all, consider how you want to brand your e-mails. A consistent look means your contacts will know what to expect. Do you want to always use your e-mails to promote sales and special bargains? Would you rather have educational newsletters where you teach something relevant to the niche? Or perhaps they're more personal, letting folks know the latest in your life and business and devoting only a small portion to offer product ideas. Some people use the combination approach and include a bit of everything.

Each approach works, but the key is to create a consistent pattern, brand, or look. Format your e-mails with your style and add new and interesting images each time, which you pin on Pinterest. This way you present yourself as professional, organized, creative, and generous—all the qualities good clients are looking for.

Below are five ideas for using your e-mail marketing list to help grow your small business on Pinterest.

1. **Provide regular updates on bargains and sales you're running with your products.** This way your clients will always know there's some way they can save money when they open your e-mail. Include images that link to Pinterest and your sales boards.

2. **Announce promotional events like contests, drawings, or free giveaways.** This instills the promise of good deals inside, but the events are designed so that the readers must take action to participate.

They must enter the contest or drawing and must do some certain thing to be eligible for the free drawing. Promote these events on Pinterest and offer more details if the viewers provide their e-mail address.

3. **Send newsletters.** These can be angled in many ways; however, one of the most attractive is to offer advice or education. This way the readers know they're going to learn something each time they open up your newsletter. Jungle Red Writers (which Roberta Isleib is part of; see Chapter 13) will consistently bring up a discussion on a writing issue (which is linked to the Jungle Red Writers' blog, where readers can make comments), provide an interview with a successful author, or even share favorite recipes. Whichever way, the readers always know they're going to get something interesting supplied by fellow writers.

   Create a "Newletters" pinboard on Pinterest with your favorite or most popular newsletters. On the pinboard make sure the viewers can easily sign up for your future newsletters by supplying their e-mail address.

4. **Run your Pinterest marketing campaigns through your e-mails.** This will vary depending on which campaign and how long it lasts, but e-mails are a great way to directly involve your contacts, who might not have any way of hearing about it otherwise.

5. **Send consolidated e-mails.** Here you provide a little bit of everything that's going on. Make sure your e-mails are attractive and have a consistent look. Then organize your information in a pattern that will become familiar to your readers. We like consistency and order, and so make sure your layout reflects you as a consistent, orderly, and professional person.

Best Practices

Let's look at some of the tools and other details you should consider when managing your e-mail marketing strategies.

- **Using autoresponders.** Autoresponders are a must-have e-mail management tool. E-mail management services, like the ones we mentioned above, allow you to prewrite e-mails and store them. You can then program the system to send these e-mails out on predetermined days. For example, after people initially sign up on your list, you can have the autoresponder send them prewritten e-mails for each of the next five days. This way you can welcome them, tell them your story, get them caught up on any campaigns or contests going on, provide special coupons, etc.

- **Choosing a personal or company voice.** As we discussed in Chapter 7, one of many choices you have regarding branding your business is whether you present yourself as an individual or a company. Whichever you decided earlier, you get to make the same choice here. For example, the e-mails you receive from Pinterest telling you that someone's started following you are signed "Ben and the Pinterest Team." This is a personal e-mail signature within a corporate setting.

  Consider how you want to present yourself within your e-mails. We recommend presenting yourself as a warm, real human being, i.e., yourself.

- **Testing the frequency of e-mails.** Many marketers ask how often they should send out e-mails. The answer will vary depending on you, your niche, and the quality of your e-mail list. One way to find out is to check your "opt-out" rate. If you send a daily e-mail and get an increase in the number of people opting out of your e-mails, try sending them less frequently. On the other hand, if you send out only one a month, try sending them more often and see if you get any increase of opt-outs. Before long you'll find your readership's maximum tolerance.

- **Including links to Pinterest and your website.** When your readers see something of interest, they can click on it and go straight to your Pinterest board or website or both. This is a great way to keep the momentum going when they read something that catches their fancy, and this is especially applicable if you're running a sale or promotional event.

- **Determining e-mail length.** This too will vary. Experiment to see what serves your needs. If you're providing education, interviews, and other more lengthy writing, you may need to have the equivalent of two to three pages of text with images. However, if you're promoting products and sales, a page or less might do the trick. Include just enough information to intrigue the reader to visit your website or Pinterest board.

- **Using the double opt-in.** It's important to be ethical in your e-mail marketing and only send e-mails to those who personally signed up. Many systems offer the double opt-in method, where the viewers sign up initially to receive your e-mails and then are sent an additional e-mail asking them to confirm their decision. This way you're sure that no one signed people up without their knowing it.

- **Not sending spam.** What is spam? Spam is rotten, and no one likes it, least of all anyone you would hope to sell something to. Spam is when you send e-mail messages to random people without their permission. Chances are you've received more than your share of these. Never buy e-mail addresses and contact these people, as this qualifies as spam. The double opt-in system is excellent for making sure you're only contacting those people who have given their permission.

The Three Ps of E-mail Marketing for Pinterest

Principle. E-mail marketing is one of your single most important online activities. Through e-mails you are in charge of when and with what content you contact your clients and prospects. This enables you to communicate with them more frequently and educate, inspire, and provide bargains.

Practice. Choose an e-mail list service for managing your contacts. Gather new e-mail addresses via one or more of the five ideas listed above. Then choose the format and style of your e-mails. Are you keeping recipients posted of sales and short-term bargains, educating them through interviews and tutorials, promoting activities such as contests, or a little bit of all of these? Present your e-mails in an organized, attractive, and professional way.

Profit. Through the steady and positive contact with your e-mails, you will develop deeper relationships and trust, and you will intrigue your readers into taking action and buying your products or services. So much of sales is the process of education, whether literally by providing tutorials or simply by letting readers know of your latest product line. E-mail is an ideal way to get the word out and increase sales.

Part 5

NO PRODUCT?
NO PROBLEM

Pinterest and the World of Nonprofits

The power of Pinterest isn't limited to the realm of business. Nonprofits, which collectively affect lives in every country on earth, have also discovered the benefits of this new form of social media. Through images and videos, Pinterest provides a way to engage viewers on a personal and very real level. It's one thing to tell people about the slaughter of innocent people in Uganda, but another to show them pictures of 10-year-old "soldiers" taken from their families and forced into killing. And yet another to show people what they can do to help improve lives forever.

Pinterest's visual platform is ideal for institutions helping millions of needy people throughout the world. Pinterest can change lives—it can save lives. It can change the world we live in, one pin at a time. Many nonprofit organizations are doing just this. The same concepts that have made Pinterest so popular in the first place—collecting and sharing images of things we love and find meaning in, discovering new things by people we trust, and being involved in a community of people that inspire one another—are exactly the same as those that will help your nonprofit thrive on Pinterest.

The marketing strategies and campaigns explained in this book can be tailored to work within the world of nonprofits. Great images are re-pinned, liked, and commented on, and those that catch a nerve go viral, taking on a life of their own as they are repinned thousands of times. The National Center for Charitable Statistics estimates that over one in four people between September 2009 and September 2010 who were over the age of 16 volunteered through or for an organization. Given the virality of Pinterest itself, the potential for how your nonprofit can expand its message is nothing short of phenomenal.

Let's look at key strategies and techniques for expanding the power of Pinterest into the world of nonprofits. We'll finish with an excellent example of a charity using Pinterest at work: charity: water.

Who's Using Pinterest

The who's who of nonprofits on Pinterest is impressive indeed: Amnesty International, UNICEF, the American Association of Retired People (AARP), the World Wildlife Fund, the Humane Society of the United States, and the list goes on. Each has a presence on Pinterest, and each is discovering how to achieve maximum benefits. Pinterest is so new that we're all in the process of discovering its potential, and these world-renowned institutions are setting the examples in the world of charity.

But it isn't just the big boys on the block who are increasing their impact. Nonprofits come in all shapes and sizes, from multibillion-dollar organizations to one-person operations. The principles we explain in this chapter will work for all of them. Whether you're fighting to stop a civil war in Africa or striving to feed one hungry child at a time in your local neighborhood, the same techniques and tools will apply.

Below we list key issues for nonprofits and describe how Pinterest-specific strategies help expand your reach.

Opportunities Within Your Assets

Many nonprofits have a huge source of Pinterest-suitable assets right at their fingertips. Image archives contain pictures and videos of the projects, stories, fund-raising campaigns, and history of your organization. This is a readymade source of material for pinboards.

For example, an institution such as World Vision, a Christian humanitarian group, began with the inspiration of one man, Bob Pierce, and is now a multibillion-dollar organization. The organization's database is teeming with images of decades of disaster relief, poverty, and injustice campaigns. From boat people adrift in the South China Sea at the end of the Vietnam War, to the Ethiopian famine in 1985, to the devastating Indonesian undersea earthquake and tsunami in 2005, World Vision was there, photographing it all. The potential for sharing these experiences, tragedies, and successes is enormous. The titles of the charity's pinboards range from "Disaster Response," to "Clean Water," to "Child Protection."

Jolkona, a quasi-charity clearinghouse where you can choose which cause you'd like to contribute to, has a "Campaigns" pinboard. On it, it details in video many of the humanitarian campaigns it's tracking. Click on any one to understand in depth where donors' dollars go. Jolkona also has inspiring boards called "Organizations We Love!," "Products That Give Back," and "Infographics." The latter clearly explain what the current issues are and how the viewer can help.

To get up and running quickly, consider using the image archive your institution already has to begin growing, educating, and inspiring followers.

Staff on the Ground

Many charities have personnel on location around the world with cameras in hand. Why not upload images of projects daily or weekly to keep donors informed of where their dollars are going to work? How inspiring for donors to see the impact of their contributions as they unfold rather than waiting for an annual statement and request for more money. Contact of this depth serves to increase commitment and activity because it makes the problems more real, as well as the solution. Each unfolds right before the viewers' eyes.

Charity: water, the organization that you'll be reading about later in our Case Study section, has a pinboard titled "Photo of the Day." Here the organization posts images from its projects across the world. Whether it's before-and-after shots of purified water in Nepal, children drinking crystal-clear water in Honduras, or villagers surrounding their first clean water source in Uganda, the viewer is transported to the scene. It's no longer just "talk"; it becomes real through the sharing of images.

Into Harm's Way

Many nonprofits have an insider's view of the most dangerous, distressing, and difficult places in the world. From raiding brothels to rescuing exploited children to tracking down Kony in 2012, international nonprofits have people on the ground in dangerous situations doing amazing work. Most people can only imagine what it would be like to grow up homeless in war-torn Sudan or scrape out a living in the slums of New Delhi.

Pinterest provides a broadcast platform to take people to places they've never been before and to see and "meet" people they would never have the chance to otherwise. Charities can easily build pinboards on specific topics and use these to transport the viewer deep into that part of the world.

Over time these boards will collect interested followers. As the number of boards and topics increases, so will the opportunity for the viewer to see what hits closest to his or her heart. What used to take complicated tracking software to determine donors' interests can now be easily tracked through followers on the pinboards. Interested parties can opt in at any time. This allows for the slow, thoughtful, and ongoing explanation of a topic or cause—and the gradual building of a list of prospective donors.

Controversial Conversations

The best charities don't just help people; they shape the cultural responses to an issue. They advocate for change and make sure that difficult topics get talked about until that change occurs. Advocacy is central to the mission of most charities.

The best way to expose hard-to-handle topics and create momentum behind movements for change is to present the topic in ways that make people stop and think. Shock them if need be.

A classic example was the effort to stop the sale of conflict, or "blood," diamonds. The outcry over blood diamonds eventually led to the 2003 Kimberley Process Act that created a certification program to prevent the sale of conflict diamonds. Pinterest didn't exist at the time, but if it had, this is how the campaign could have been handled:

- Pictures could have been posted of the victims of abuse in the diamond trade. Many children had their hands amputated as a form of punishment. A pinboard depicting this would have had emotional impact.

- Images of beautiful diamonds could have been pinned with descriptions explaining the lives lost and hardship experienced in order to get them to market. If people learned to associate those blood diamonds with the deaths of disadvantaged and abused people, maybe they would think twice about purchasing more.

- Infographics could have been created explaining the path that blood diamonds take from deadly mines to posh Rodeo Drive shops.

- Pin-torials could have been created to help viewers identify which are "clean" diamonds and which are not.

- Call-to-action pinboards could have been created to help viewers understand what actions they could take to put a stop to the blood diamond trade.

Current campaigns against injustice and abuse can use the same techniques and ideas described above. The key is to use compelling, truthful images to tell the story. Educating viewers to all angles of the problem will help encourage them to take action more quickly. Pinterest, with its unique visual interface, is perfect for this job.

Fund-Raising

Fund-raising is core to any nonprofit's activities. Money and time help further the charity's mission, while simultaneously giving donors a sense of fulfillment and excitement at seeing the world change as a result of their generosity. Pinterest provides an excellent platform for promoting fund-raising. This can take shape in two forms: time and money.

Calls to Action for Donating Time

Millions of Americans volunteer their time to nonprofit organizations every year, and this is a driving force behind many societal improvements. Calls to action through Pinterest for donating time can take several forms.

On individual campaign boards, include pins that ask for volunteers. As the purpose of the charity campaign is spelled out, it's natural to ask for help. Link the pin to your home website where they can sign up. On the pin you can be detailed or brief; just make it clear that volunteers are needed and that this is where the viewer can go to help. The end result of a successful campaign is to inspire people to contribute in whatever way they can.

Create specific "Volunteer Here" pinboards. Pin infographics about what volunteers would do, how much time it would take, and what the end results would be. Always let them know the impact they'll have when they give their time. Include before-and-after images, testimonials, or whatever educational pins would work in your specific situation.

Calls to Action for Donating Money

Calls to action for donating money are a natural setup on Pinterest. The price banner functionality works just as well for charitable donations as it does for retail sales. Many charities are using just this tool for their fund-raising campaigns.

Operation Smile suggests a donation amount in its pinboard tagline, as you can see in Figure 17.1. Other charities, such as World Vision, display fund-raising merchandise with Pinterest price banners. Both are useful calls to action for potential contributors. Consider also adding your phone number to your board tagline.

Finding New Followers

Many of the same techniques for gaining new followers for a small business work equally as well for nonprofits. Pinterest isn't just a place to solicit donations and catalyze enthusiasm for issues; it's also ideal for

Figure 17.1 Operation Smile suggests a gift amount in its pinboard tagline explaining the time and result—$240 and 45 minutes to change a life.

coordinating word-of-mouth campaigns. After all, one of the core drivers of Pinterest is learning about new ideas and inspirations from people you trust.

Elements of a good word-of-mouth campaign on Pinterest include the following:

- Educating your followers on the problem issue through pictures, infographics, videos, and details of how people are being affected.

- Creating pinboards stating what's needed from volunteers and how that will positively impact lives. The more detail the better. Tell your story through excellent images.

- Committing to continually update and expand your Pinterest presence and become an active member of the community. Results need to be measured, monitored, and managed.

- Constructing pinboards that state credible goals: "Gathering 10,000 blood diamond activists by January 1st " or "Raising $25,000 for new smiles this summer."

- Getting creative. The World Wildlife Fund has a pinboard with animal e-cards to send out. People love fun things, and the more you engage people in doing them, the more they'll help you spread the word.

- Infusing a sense of urgency in your message. Let the viewer know what will happen if the money isn't raised or volunteer time isn't donated.

- Keeping your followers updated. Let them be involved in your progress and reward them for helping with time or money. When people know that they really are making a difference, they're more likely to actively get other people involved.

Case Study—charity: water

Charity: water (http://www.charitywater.org) brings clean-water solutions to developing nations throughout the world. In the organization's words, "When Scott Harrison threw a party for his thirty-first birthday, he asked everyone to bring $20 instead of gifts. He used 100 percent of that money to fund six wells in northern Uganda. When the projects were complete, everyone who attended the party received photos and GPS coordinates so they could see their impact. We've been doing that ever since. One hundred percent of all public donations directly fund water projects. We track every dollar, and when the projects are complete, we show our supporters their impact."

The folks at charity: water began experimenting with Pinterest in early 2011, but as with many in those early days, they weren't quite sure what to do with this new beast.

"At first we weren't sure how a nonprofit would fit into the Pinterest community. But we followed Paull's motto (our Director of Digital Engagement) of 'Keep it simple and do it wrong quickly' and jumped in. It quickly became clear that Pinterest was a natural fit for sharing all our different visuals in one place—photography, videos, infographics, etc. Our founder likes to say 'We show, not tell.' We show the impact of clean water, not through statistics or numbers, but through individual lives and images."

And it seems to be working. Charity: water is seeing an increase in referral traffic from Pinterest, and people are pinning images from the organization's website in return. The same cycle that happens with businesses—traffic from your website to Pinterest and then back to your website—works with nonprofits too. It's a matter of getting your message across visually, and charity: water is a perfect fit.

Best Practices

Below are several of charity: water's best practices:

- Start simple. Watch who's repinning your content and where it's going. Learn what viewers like.

- Don't be afraid to try different strategies. See what does and doesn't work for your brand.

- Stay on top of the latest changes and features that Pinterest puts out. The website is new and growing, and updated features are common.

- Like and comment on other people's pins. Be active.

- Pin regularly, but not too much and not too little. Keep your followers rewarded but not overwhelmed.

- Use catchy descriptions that are searchable.

This sounds a lot like best practices for businesses, doesn't it? You can approach this entire book as one big Pinterest marketing campaign for your nonprofit. Imagine the changes you could realize.

Seven Keys to Pinterest for Nonprofits

Many of the business marketing techniques we've been discussing will work equally well for your nonprofit. Others just need to be tailored a bit. Check out the following seven keys to success:

1. **Know your donor.** Understand clearly who your target audience is and pin images and content for them. If you were a potential contributor to your own charity, what kinds of images would get your heart racing?

2. **Get up close and personal.** No one wants to skim through images that look like advertisements. Let your followers know the details, good, bad, and ugly. Now's not the time to tiptoe around the serious issues. Impress; startle; motivate.

3. **Pin images of the people directly impacted by your charity.** Tell their stories through pictures and through videos. Take your followers on a journey to the other side of the world where they can make a difference.

4. **Set achievable goals.** Make your goals clear and real and show the viewer what the end result will look like.

5. **Ask for help.** Use calls to action for time and money. Get creative.

6. **Be part of the Pinterest community.** Repin, like, and comment on other nonprofits' images and pinboards and those of the public itself. Be an active contributor to your online community.

7. **Use the marketing tools and techniques from this book.** Add Pin It and Follow Me On Pinterest buttons. Study and learn from your most repinned images and articles. In other words, treat your nonprofit's marketing campaign like a business's one. The only difference is how you measure success.

Influencing Your Community with Pinterest

*T*he power of Pinterest extends into lands far beyond the every-day business world. You saw in Chapter 17 that Pinterest can help the world in many powerful ways—even in communities on the other side of the planet. In this chapter we'll look at ways Pinterest can help closer to home. Many of us are involved in our communities in either a volunteer or paying capacity, and yet finding ways to activate members, citizens, and every-now-and-then participants brings on an entirely new set of challenges. It takes looking at the situation from a somewhat different perspective.

The distinct advantage you'll be working from is that we're already in the second decade of the twenty-first century. E-mail, cell phones, and, yes, social media are all commonplace. Most people are hooked up online, and you can easily communicate with them in bulk. This is a far cry from working an endless telephone list or knocking on door after door. The key is to target your goals and message correctly.

Pinterest, with its visual, user-friendly format, is ideal for reaching out to your local community. Whether a government, school, church, or Boy Scout troop, you can develop outreach campaigns that will help activate your followers and generate new members. Goal-oriented projects, whether building a new community pool, opening a new 4-H branch, or selling tickets to the school play, can all be broadcast and celebrated through Pinterest. The approach is slightly different from that for growing sales, but enough similarities exist that the basic process will appear easy and intuitive.

Similarities and Differences with Business Tactics

The ideas behind "growing" your community and growing your business aren't that far apart. Let's start with the similarities, which are pretty straightforward: The more exposure you have, the better. Reaching out regularly to your contacts with ideas, education, and great deals helps strengthen the relationship and trust; the more trust you have, the more involvement you'll achieve. Allowing your followers an inside look at you as a person through images on Pinterest helps them grow closer; the more real you are to them, and the more values you share, the more activity you'll see.

Sounds just like growing your small business through Pinterest, doesn't it? All those tactics equally apply to expanding your reach throughout your community too. And each of these qualities is easily achievable through Pinterest and the integrated marketing strategies you've learned here so far.

As for differences, a major one is that no tangible product exists, although we learned that this isn't all that important (see Chapter 13). Instead, you must activate people who might or might not have a strong motivation to help out; and these same people also might not be qualified to do what you're asking—their areas of expertise may lie in completely different areas. For example, let's say you're fund-raising for new marching band uniforms and the group of volunteers you have to select from consists of a retired farmer, a 16-year-old getting extra credit after skipping class, and a new bank manager just relocated from the city.

None of the differences between reaching out to your community and growing your business present insurmountable problems. Each can be tackled in its own, unique way, with the end result being that Pinterest shines equally as bright in your town or city as it does within your business.

Where to Start

The primary goal of almost any community program is mobilizing people into action of some sort. However, mobilizing diverse sets of people with varying degrees of motivation can be challenging and re-quires a distinct approach. Outwardly the goal appears the same as in business—to get people to act. But within a community it can be more difficult to inspire action. When we say "community," this can refer to any nonprofit or volunteer group. It could be your church, the city coun-cil, a shelter for the homeless, or your work with Habitat for Humanity.

Let's look at several steps you can take to increase motivation and therefore activity within the community setting:

- First among these is establishing the value of the goal. You need to clearly show how members of the community will benefit and how important the viewers' help is. To do this, create pinboards to show the end result: kids swimming in the new Olympic-size pool, the marching band in the Fourth of July parade, or the church choir performing at the Christmas concert.

- Find other leaders within your community and enlist their time and effort. No one person can do it all, and that includes you. Your goal here is to inspire others to help. One thing that will help enor-mously in finding leaders is for you to already have a certain level of professionalism and activity in the works. Here is where Pin-terest and other social media platforms can really help. By build-ing a beautiful Pinterest profile and pinboards, by integrating your community's other social media networks, and by having at least the makings of a solid e-mail campaign in place, you show you're ready for business. Then get the word out that you're look-ing for committee chairs, project coordinators, and the like. People will much more easily follow those who are already moving than they will those who are standing still.

- After finding new leaders to help you spread the message, ask them to form their own groups of followers for the same goal. Have them use your Pinterest and social media efforts as models.

- What tools will your helpers and followers need to get your project completed? Think through this and find ways to make them available. Or else make their acquisition part of the project itself. You can create pinboards showing the various stages, what's needed, what each will lead to, and you can end with images of the final goal. This is an excellent way to inspire people.

- In the same line of thinking as above, will your helpers need any extra training? If so, create tutorials or videos and post them on Pinterest.

- Measure your results and share them with everybody. The importance of this one step cannot be overstated. People love to see progress and know that their time and energy is paying off. Keep track of the progress of your goal(s) and let people know.

- Document what you've done so that you can do it again, or share your findings with those that come after you.

Next let's look at five different examples of how different communities can use Pinterest to market their efforts.

Churches

Mars Hill Church, based in Seattle, recently discovered the power of Pinterest. Churches as a whole don't have much money for marketing, and so social media has become an ideal way to fill this need. Mars Hill found that once it began building pinboards that appealed to its broad demographics, women especially, the number of followers increased, as did referrals to its website. (See Figure 18.1.)

Jake Johnson, Director of Content Strategy for Mars Hill Church, notes:

> After reading some articles on how businesses were using the service [Pinterest], and through some discussions with colleagues, I began to think through how it might be useful for our content marketing at Mars Hill Church. Once I dug in, I was impressed with the growth of the platform and intrigued by its visual focus. . . . Additionally, I knew the users of Pinterest were overwhelmingly female and I wanted to use that opportunity to

Mars Hill Church
Pinned 16 weeks ago via **pinmarklet**

⇅ Repin   ♥ Like   From marshill.com

11 Stories Of Jesus Working At Mars Hill Church In 2011
Pinned via **pinmarklet**

Figure 18.1 A Mars Hill Church pin—clean, concise, and appealing to women.

speak well to the women of Mars Hill and to women who engage with our content.

At Mars Hill the staff created pinboards with a wide array of topics and found that the keys to success with Pinterest are very much like what we've been discussing already for businesses:

- Think visually. Pin dynamic, repinnable images that get your core message across.

- Create content that stands on its own. In other words, each pin tells its own story and has its own message within the larger whole.

- Pin gradually, over time. Don't inundate your followers with images.

- Pin regularly.

- Measure your results. Use Google Analytics and other services to see which images are driving traffic and what your overall Pinterest numbers are. Do more of what works and less of what doesn't.

Jake Johnson described the church's use of Pinterest this way:

> Our first priority at Mars Hill Church, as always, is to talk about Jesus. We view all our online efforts as evangelical ones and want to steward well the significant platform God has blessed us with to preach the gospel. As such, our first and most prominent boards are the "Jesus" board—which is fun because when people follow it, a message says so and so is "following Jesus"— and the "Gospel" board.
>
> Additionally, we're highlighting events, design, sermon series, music, books, and dovetailing in support of our current sermon series, Real Marriage, with content applicable for men, women, couples, singles, and parents. I feel strongly that Pinterest will force organizations to up their game on design, as it's such a visual platform. In order to get noticed, you have to have great photography and art. Organizations that want to gain traction should start making design a significant part of their content strategy so that when there is good content to share there is a good image to pin associated with it.

High Schools and College Planning

Pinterest for schools works from two angles: (1) schools wanting to communicate with students and (2) students looking for information about schools. Let's look at both sides.

Many colleges have tapped into the Pinterest phenomenon and are building more and more attractive Pinterest profiles. While this is a relatively new vehicle for increasing exposure, the results are impressive. In Figure 18.2, showing Drake University's Pinterest profile, notice how the pinboards aren't about readin', writin', and 'rithmetic, but rather about campus life, the kind of fun the student can expect, and the overall feel of the institute. "Rad Room Decor" and "Ran Out of Bulldog Bucks?" (recipes for when you're really broke) are a couple of pinboard examples.

When building your college or high school Pinterest board, make sure you put yourself into a prospective student's shoes. What would a prospective student find fun and interesting (that you can pin on a public board)? What's your school's main focus: music, engineering,

Figure 18.2 Drake University's profile gives a fun and exciting feel.

business? What kind of sports and clubs can students join? Try to represent the overall feel of your school through the images you pin.

On the other side of the coin, Pinterest is a great tool for high school students and their parents checking out which colleges to apply to. Figure 18.3 shows a pinboard called "Highschoogle" filled with facts and information about how to hunt down and apply to the best colleges.

Figure 18.3 Highschoogle, part of independent publisher People Tested, provides advice and information on college searches. (http://www.highschoogle.com)

To find a school on Pinterest, just type in its name in the search box and see what comes up. It's amazing how the feel of the place so easily comes across in the images the school chooses to post.

Sororities and fraternities also use Pinterest to celebrate their causes. If you're considering joining one of these or want to catch up on what's happening with the alumni, Pinterest is a great place to search.

Local Sports Teams

Local sports teams have a huge opportunity to benefit from the popularity and visual appeal of Pinterest. For example, let's look at what your local middle school's girls' soccer team could do:

- Create a "Game Schedule" pinboard. For away games, include driving instructions, advice on where to park, and local eateries.

- Create a "Tips and Inspiration" pinboard. Include soccer advice and wisdom as well as inspirational quotes and videos.

- Include videos of games and spectacular moments. You can also include coach talks, training clips, and fans.

- Create a "Pictures" board. Here you post fun and inspiring images of players, their families, and fans. People love to receive recognition, even if it's just for showing up in the rain. Give thanks to your team members and supporters here. Consider making this a collaborative board where others can contribute.

- If you're supercompetitive, you can even create a "Scouting" board. Include images and videos of your competitors' teams, plays, and players. Use it as an educational tool so that your viewers can learn each team's strong and weak points.

Community and Government Organizations

Whether you're the local Boy or Girl Scouts leader, head of the city council, or the mayor running for another term, Pinterest can play a valuable role. As with each of the other examples, build pinboards stating a clear vision of who you are, what you stand for, and what your goals are. Appeal to your followers' emotions through strong images and educate them in your cause through tutorials, infographics, and videos.

If you're running for your second term as mayor, maybe you want to create a board explaining why that construction on Main Street has been going on all summer long. Pin before-and-after images, and educate your viewers about why it was important to do the construction now, in the middle of school vacation. This effort at connecting with your constituents is unique and shows you care. It'll set you apart from the crowd in no time.

If you're part of the local scout troop (or any other charity or community program), create a "Leaders" board, highlighting your Eagle Scouts or those who have achieved new badges. Create boards chronicling the year's events, and remember to include lots of pictures of individuals and their families. Get as many people involved as you can—they love it. If you brought in an expert on say, knot tying, add educational boards and infographics on what everyone learned.

In short, every community can benefit from the bonding that occurs when images and enthusiasm are shared in the Pinterest environment. Explain what's been happening and what your plans are for the future, and bring people along in your passion and cause. There's room for everyone.

A Community Marketing Campaign

Below we outline eight steps for successfully conducting a community marketing campaign on Pinterest. Tailor these to whichever community service you're involved in, whether for your church, city council, Rotary Club, or . . . The principles are the same, and all lead toward mobilizing your members to action on behalf of the group as a whole—the primary goal of any community marketing campaign.

1. Create a pinboard that serves as a "base camp" for your message. It's from here that you'll launch the campaign. Give it a clear title— "Midvale Summer Girls Camp," "Shelter from the Storm Fund-Raiser," "Midsummer Night's Eve—Oakland Community Playhouse," and the like—and pin images of the end goal. Introduce key individuals and inspirational messages.

2. Share your vision with other members of your team. Make sure they understand what your goals are and what you expect to achieve through your Pinterest and other social media marketing efforts. Ask them to expand the message into their social media

circles. This one step is amazingly powerful, as it truly brings so-cial commerce into play—community style.

3. Clearly state your project goals and deadline(s) and create a pin-board displaying them. Is it to fund-raise $10,000 within six months? $100,000? Maybe you need to sell 500 tickets to the play, or perhaps you need 30 volunteers for the women's shel-ter. Let followers know what you need and why. Appeal to them on an emotional level so that they understand why you're doing what you're doing and what good their involvement would bring.

4. Set goals for community involvement. For example, with your team's efforts you could try to get 1,000 Pinterest followers within a month. Tailor your goals to your community's size and the scope of your project.

5. Track and display your progress. If you have 700 new followers on Pinterest but need another 300, let folks know! If you're halfway to your fund-raising goal, let them know the good news, that you've made progress and also that the work isn't over yet. People want to know their efforts aren't for nothing. Build team spirit and energy by including everyone in the vision, goals, and progress.

6. Ask people to report back to you on how much impact they're hav-ing in their own social media circles. Add these numbers to the overall progress reports noted above.

7. Celebrate and give credit. When you achieve your goals, or even if you don't but have made progress by the deadline, stop and give thanks and credit to those who helped you. Honor their efforts and point out those who did spectacularly well. Without their help you wouldn't have made as much headway.

8. Record your results and what you learned. Share these on a pin-board as yet one more way to bring your community together.

The Three Ps of Influencing Your Community with Pinterest

Principle. Community projects can be deeply enhanced through the use of Pinterest. The proper use of pinboards will educate, inspire, and motivate your followers and their friends and families. In this way you can expand the reach and ease of achieving your community goals.

Practice. Whatever your project and community—church, government, school, sports team, community volunteer—follow the advice and steps above to get community members involved. Clearly state who you are and what your project is about, and let them know your end goals and why it will make their community a better place to live. Appeal to your viewers' emotions and sense of belonging, and they will become energized to help. Run an outright community campaign by following the eight steps above.

Profit. Here the term is used figuratively. Your "profit" will arrive in the form of achieving project goals through the mobilization of fellow community members. Strength comes in numbers, and the more people you have helping you, the more you'll get done. Your images and campaigns through Pinterest will educate and inspire people to give you a hand.

Marketing and Technology Resources

*I*t seems that as soon as a new piece of technology comes out, an avalanche of clever and useful add-ons, plug-ins, and applications turn up. In a sense it's true. The age we live in means a lot of very bright people have access to tools that can make all our lives easier and more efficient. The issue then becomes sifting through the cool new gadgets and widgets to see which really work. Some of us are naturals at this, always trying out new things and downloading the latest apps. Others let their friends do the beta testing and then jump onto whatever functioned the best.

In this chapter we're going to be that trusted friend and walk you through the various options you have to amplify your Pinterest experience with outside technology. Many of these will directly affect your marketing efforts, especially those that have to do with tracking your Pinterest activity, such as Curalate, Pinreach, and Google Analytics. Other applications are simply catchy tools that make it easier and faster to pin, view your pins, and learn more about where they were pinned from.

As your business grows with Pinterest, you'll be utilizing most every aspect of the platform, and you'll probably be eager to see what else is available. This may not occur at the beginning, but it will along the way. So see what's available, what you can apply now, and what might be better saved for the future. And remember, technology changes, and what's working today may be overshadowed by something better tomorrow. None of these products or services are Pinterest supported or approved, and so apply your own due diligence, educate yourself, and give them a try.

Image-Editing Tools

Several chapters have emphasized the advantages of enhancing your images for the dual purposes of making them more likely to be pinned and embedding your brand. That's all good and well, but the question inevitably arises, "How the heck do I do that?" Fortunately, image-editing tools exist that make it relatively easy to enhance your images any way you like.

With somewhat of a learning curve, but nothing terminal, you'll be able to embed your logo and website in your images and create attractive borders, as Courtney Slazinik explained in Chapter 11. You'll be able to create infographics, advertorials, and how-to pins, as we emphasized in Chapter 10. As well, free services are available that help you create virtual invitations, contest announcements, and promotional materials for most any marketing campaign that will make you look like you're a pro. After all, you're well on your way to becoming one.

Photoshop Elements

This is the granddaddy of all image-editing tools, and if you pick just one, make it this one. Photoshop Elements is the simpler and much cheaper version of Adobe Photoshop, and you'll be able to unleash your creative self with very little training. The software can be downloaded online and runs well on both PCs and Macs. As with all these programs, to get started on Photoshop Elements or learn more, just Google it.

Most important, many free training resources are available. Google the site, and you have instant access to several, but you can also visit YouTube for a plethora of extra training. These are all free. You can also subscribe to *Photoshop Elements Techniques* magazine and get Photoshop's own training.

As with so many of these programs, and especially if the thought of having to learn how to edit your photos makes you want to rip your hair out before you've even started, remember to take it step-by-step. Upload a few pictures and just *play*. Don't worry about creating fine art in your first session; just get the feel for your options. Over time you'll gain confidence and begin to apply what you've learned to your Pinterest images. Remember to have fun!

Pinstamatic.com

This free service offers some interesting options. With very little effort you can create full web pages, make sticky notes, share your Spotify track, write a quote with several choices for backgrounds, share your Twitter profile, create a cool-looking calendar date, or add a Google map with the location marked and included in the description.

In all, these are practical, fun, and quick Pinterest-specific options that have virtually no learning curve. With all of them, be sure to add a link to your website or blog so that you're always working toward directing traffic to your site.

TRAFFIC TIP

Many free photo-editing software programs exist online. Just type in "free image-editing tools" on Google and see the choices that come up. Photoscape, Picnic, and Gimp consistently get positive reviews, as do several others. Check them out, and see what's currently being recommended. This is a great way to get started for free.

Paperless Post

For online invitations and stationery, this is a fast and easy go-to source. It provides a wide selection of backgrounds and styles, and many are free; the rest you purchase for minimal cost. The cool thing is that all the work is done for you. Choose a background or upload one of your own photos. Select a font and write in the details, and you're done!

It couldn't be easier. Use these to launch Pinterest contests, campaigns, giveaways, or anything else that fits your marketing fancy. Remember to add a link in the pin so that when the image is clicked on, the viewer will be taken to your website or blog.

ShareAsImage

How do people get those cool-looking quotes up on Pinterest? Many of them use ShareAsImage.com. Previously known as PinAQuote, this service allows you to highlight text from any website and turn it into an attractive pin. As far as your Pinterest marketing efforts go, the best way to do this is to pin a quote from your own blog or website. This way the viewers will be taken directly back to where you want them—your site! If you pin a quote from somewhere else, be sure and give the original source the credit.

Free Traffic Analysis Tools

We've mentioned several times in this book the importance of tracking your progress with Pinterest. You cannot manage your marketing endeavors effectively if you cannot track your results. It's as simple as that. You must be able to see what's bringing in more traffic and causing more sales. The more you understand how your business works, the exponentially greater your chances for success. Learn which pins are creating the most traffic, and then compare them for similarities. Which marketing campaign is bringing in the most new prospects, and how many of those convert to sales? For example, if you run three contests over a six-month period, you must know which one worked the best and why. Because guess what? This means you can do more similar to that one and skip the less effective contests.

You grow what you can measure, and so learn to measure your business. The good news is, it's easy. Many free and paying services exist with the sole purpose of helping you track traffic.

We'll look at the free services first. As with other technologies and applications in this chapter, be sure and check out each of these for yourself. They change over time, and new ones will rise to overtake them. But this is a great place to get started tracking your success.

Google Analytics

This service is essential for anyone running a website or blog—that would be the vast majority of you. From here you can learn how much traffic is coming in from Pinterest and compare that with the number of visitors from other sites. You'll be able to tell how many referral links come from Pinterest and then even how much traffic comes in per link. This will help you identify your most impactful pins.

As you launch your campaigns, you'll be able to closely monitor any increase in traffic and see where it came from. This is exactly the type of data you need to determine which pins and campaigns are bringing in the most people.

With each visit recorded, you can drill down and learn the number of site pages that are visited and the average duration of each visit. You'll also be able to tell, pin by pin, the percentage of new versus repeat visits. You will be able to find which pins, campaigns, or other marketing tactics bring in people. This knowledge carries with it the power to change your Pinterest marketing for the better. And all for free.

Pinreach

This free and simple service provides valuable data within the specific world of Pinterest. With just a few clicks of the mouse, you can see which of your boards and pins are the most popular regarding repins, likes, followers, and comments. You're provided with a general stats board giving your overall number of repins, etc., as well as a ranking number. The latter allows you to compare your impact on Pinterest with that of other users.

Pinreach gives you a good idea of your reach within the Pinterest community that Google Analytics does not. However, it does not provide any information about incoming or outgoing Pinterest traffic. Therefore, use this in combination with Google Analytics.

One interesting aspect of this service is that it tracks Trending Pins and Trending Members. Here you can see which pins are taking off and which members are having the most influence. Check these out to see what you can learn.

Pinpuff

This is another Pinterest-specific service much like Pinreach that tracks your influence within Pinterest. Although not as comprehensive as Pinreach, it does provide three scores—Reach, Activity, and Virility. It then offers brief bits of advice about how to improve your scores. For example, maybe you need to pin more images each day or reach out to other social media sites for more traffic.

TRAFFIC TIP

Pintics and Pinerly are two additional Pinterest-specific analysis tools for managing your Pinterest influence. As with Pinreach and Pinpuff, as of now you can't see the inflow and outflow of traffic to and from Pinterest, but you can get a much closer handle on your impact within the Pinterest community. Both Pintics and Pinerly are in beta versions, but watch these as they grow.

Curalate

Sometimes it pays to upgrade to industrial-strength analytical tools. Curalate is one such example. So far, this service provides the most comprehensive tools for measuring and monitoring your presence on Pinterest. The Curalate philosophy is that your brand presence comes from two sources—your brand itself and your brand's fans. No other service allows you to track what your fans are doing on Pinterest. Curalate has filled this need. (See Figure 19.1.)

What's key here is that your fans will collectively share more about your brand than you will yourself. Therefore, it's a huge advantage to be able to understand these metrics and adjust your marketing strategies to nurture your fans. Curalate uses a sophisticated selection of image recognition algorithms to continuously sort Pinterest data. It's able to track how the content from your pinboards and website is being distributed throughout Pinterest. You'll learn who's most active and with which of your images.

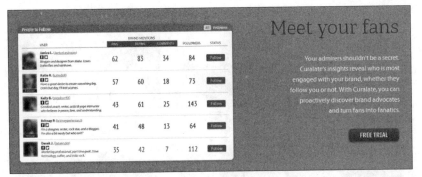

Figure 19.1 Curalate helps you understand and manage the influence of your brand's fans.

As of this writing, Curalate is still in a private beta version with the intention of launching publicly soon and with a limited number of free trials. But it does have pay versions and will likely have more free trials over time.

Google Chrome Browser Extensions

Browser extensions are downloadable programs that allow you to do things with your Internet browser you previously couldn't. In the context of Pinterest, several free extensions exist that give you cool tools to manage your pins and searches. As of this writing, most of these extensions exist for Google Chrome (as opposed to Internet Explorer, Apple's Safari, Mozilla Firefox, etc.). Over time this will change, but let's look at what's available now.

To access the extensions, just Google their name along with the keywords *Google chrome extension*.

Pinterest Image Expander, Pinterest Zoom, and Pinzy

After installing one of these free extensions, hover your mouse over any Pinterest image and watch it automatically zoom closer. This is a fast and easy way to get a better look at an image you might want to repin. See Figure 19.2.

Figure 19.2 With Google Chrome's image expander extension, you can zoom up any image by hovering your mouse.

Pinterest Right Click

This handy application allows you to right-click with your mouse and bring up the Pin It button. This is just a fast way of being able to pin without having to go to Pinterest itself or use the bookmarked Pin It button.

Pinterest Recent Activity Expander

Here you're able to enlarge the thumbnail images that appear in your Recent Activity feed along the left-hand side of your Pinners You Follow page. This is a fast way to see exactly which image was repinned.

Pin Search

This extension will add a new button called *Search* onto each pin. It will appear next to your choices to repin and like. When you click on Search, you'll be taken to the Google search page where this same image can be found. You can research where it came from and where else it appears. This is different from the link embedded within the pinned image. Instead, it's as if you've just Googled the image. This is a great tool for seeing where else your own images might be appearing on the Internet.

Pinterest Pro

This extension is a one-stop shop for many of the extensions mentioned above. If you want them all, simply download Pinterest Pro, and you'll be able to enlarge images or right-click to pin. It also features a clever Popular Pin button that brings up a list of popular pins on Pinterest. This is a great way to stay on top of what's hot.

Pop-Up E-mail Capture Tool

As we saw in Chapter 16, several ways exist to build your marketing e-mail address list. One of these is to install a pop-up e-mail capture tool. When new visitors try to access your site, a pop-up box will appear, and they must sign up (i.e., give you at least their e-mail address) before they can enter your site and view the content.

This is called an interruption-marketing tactic and isn't for everyone, because, as the term implies, you interrupt the viewers and bring them to a stop until they give you their data. However, the results with this technique are excellent. You will collect many more e-mail addresses using this tool. To soften it, you can offer something free in exchange: a special report, an e-mail newsletter, or the ability to download your free e-book.

A popular software package is Pop Up Domination. It's simple and easy to use. It can be found at http://www.popupdomination.com.

Webinars

You'll recall from Chapter 16 that we discussed the value of webinars as a great way to build your e-mail lists. The idea is to promote your webinar on your website and then create images to pin on Pinterest with the relevant details. As your webinar pin gets repinned, be sure and comment and like those repins to build your community.

Webinars are live presentations where you share your computer screen with viewers and are simultaneously on a conference call. Webinars can also be recorded, and you can later sell them for a reduced price, give them away as a prize, etc.

Currently, one of the best webinar services is anymeeting.com (previously called freebinar.com). As its name implies, it's free for basic webinar setups and services. Bells and whistles cost a modest monthly fee. Many other services have free trial periods, which is a great way to compare companies and see which one you'd like to make a commitment to if webinars are part of your overall marketing strategy. Check out webex.com and gotomeeting.com for starters.

Lead-Capturing Landing Pages

Another great tool for building your e-mail list is with landing pages. These can be incorporated into your current website or blog or used as independent one-page websites. As we mentioned in Chapter 16, landing pages can be used in conjunction with contests to allow entrants to register in exchange for giving you their e-mail address. You can also use landing pages to gather e-mail addresses in exchange for a free e-book, newsletter, chance to enter a giveaway, or whatever else your marketing genius comes up with. You can even develop a landing page to simply close the sale.

As with webinars, many companies exist that can help you set up a landing page. Check out instapage.com for something simple and inexpensive. At the moment, kickofflabs.com offers landing pages for free.

General Resources

It's important to stay on top of the latest trends and technologies regarding marketing and building your business on Pinterest. A great way to do this is to visit us on http://www.pinterestpower.com. You'll find the latest tools and tips and cool new ideas for building your business through Pinterest. You can also visit Jason's blog at http://www.marketing onpinterest.com.

Notes

Chapter 1

p. 4 "Pinterest allows you to organize and share all the beautiful things you find on the web.": http://www.pinterest.com.

p. 5 "As a visual brand where images and ideas are so central to what we do, we are extremely excited about Pinterest. This is a tremendous complement.": Gayle Butler quoted in Bill Mikey, "Better Homes and Gardens Goes Big with Pinterest," *Better Homes and Gardens*, March 8, 2012.

Chapter 3

p. 27 "Most everyone is proud of some aspect of their life, whether it's the furniture in their house, or it's the clothes they wear every day . . .": Ben Silbermann, quoted in Rony El-Nashar, *Ben Silbermann Cofounder of Pinterest Retells His Story*, March 11, 2012; http://cofounder.tv/videos/ben -silbermann-cofounder-pinterest-story.

p. 28 "Let's let people express themselves in a way that is true and authentic to who they are. And let's let people discover things not through any other means than through their friends and other people.": Ben Silbermann, *Pinterest CEO, Ben Silbermann, speaking at Startup Grin*; http://www.youtube .com/watch?v=1JLc2PYyCa0.

p. 29 "Midwestern moms and Mormons.": ibid.

p. 30 "Part of the mission of Pinterest is actually to get you off the site and inspire you to do things you otherwise wouldn't have the confidence to do.": ibid.

Chapter 6

p. 54 "What you learn about a person through their collections is very true to who they are.": Ben Silbermann, *Ben Silbermann: Collecting and the Everyday Tastemaker*; http://fora.tv/2010/11/05/Ben_Silbermann_Collecting_and _the_Everyday_Tastemaker.

Chapter 8

p. 79 From home-based startups to Fortune 500 behemoths, most businesses have a social media presence; yet a recent study by Insites Consulting found that only 16 percent felt they had fully integrated their social media presences . . . : Insites Consulting press release, February 12, 2011.

p. 82 With over 845 million users [. . .] and still growing, this is the site that comes to mind when we hear about social media: *Facebook Stats*, February 2012; http://en.wikipedia.org/wiki/Facebook_statistics.

Chapter 9

p. 93 "Data on Twitter showed that tweets done at 4 p.m. EST received the most amount of retweets . . .": Dan Zarrella, *When's the Best Time to Publish Blog Posts*, December 6, 2010; http://www.problogger.net/archives/2010/12/06 /whens-the-best-time-to-publish-blog-posts. Also at http://www.dan zarrella.com.

p. 93 The best times to pin on Pinterest are between 2 and 4 p.m. and between 8 p.m. and 1 a.m. EST. (By "best times" we mean the times that give you an edge on the number of repins.) . . .: Jason Keith, *Pinterest Marketing Stats (Infographic)*, April 9, 2012; http://socialfresh.com/pinterest-info- graphic.

p. 93 However, according to Bit.ly.com's chief scientist, Hilary Mason, the best time to pin is Saturday morning.: Peter Pachal, *Here's the Best Time to Share on Pinterest*, May 5, 2012; http://mashable.com/2012/05/05/best-time -pinterest.

Chapter 12

p. 129 "If I had to guess, social commerce is the next area to really blow up.": Mark Zuckerberg, quoted in David Rowan and Tom Cheshire, *Commerce Gets So- cial: How Social Networks Are Driving What You Buy*, January 18, 2011; http:// www.wired.co.uk/magazine/archive/2011/02/features/social-networks -drive-commerce?page=all.

p. 131 "We want to be inspired by people's ideas and to enable them to take an active part in helping us shape not only the future of Nestlé Marketplace

[Nestlé's online store], but also of our products . . .": Gerhard Berssenbrügge, quoted in Lauren Fisher, *Social Commerce: How Money Is
Changing Social Media*, September 6, 2011; http://thenextweb.com
/socialmedia/2011/09/06/social-commerce-how-money-is-changing
-social-media.

Chapter 13

p. 138 "In 2003, Jane began the task of creating a unique meal planning service
that would incorporate all of the things that a mom would want to take the
stress out of dinnertime . . .": *The eMeals Story*; http://emeals.com/emeals
-story.

Chapter 14

p. 155 "Etsy is the world's handmade marketplace.": http://www.etsy.com/.

p. 155 Fourteen million registered users have set up over 800,000 'shops,' the
Etsy term for seller accounts.: Max Chafkin, *Can Rob Kalin Scale Etsy?*, April
2011; http://www.inc.com/magazine/20110401/can-rob-kalin-scale
-etsy.html.

Chapter 17

p. 192 Charity: water brings clean-water solutions to developing nations
throughout the world.: http://www.charitywater.org.

Chapter 18

p. 198 "After reading some articles on how businesses were using the service
[Pinterest], and through some discussions with colleagues, I began to
think through how it might be useful for our content marketing at Mars
Hill Church . . .": Jake Johnson, Mars Hill Church.

p. 200 "Our first priority at Mars Hill Church, as always, is to talk about Jesus. We
view all our online efforts as evangelical ones and want to steward well the
significant platform God has blessed us with to preach the gospel . . .": Jake
Johnson, Mars Hill Church.

Index

About the Authors

Jason Miles is the vice president of advancement (marketing, fundraising, and human resources) at Northwest University in Seattle, Washington. He holds a master's degree in business administration and undergraduate degrees in both organizational management and biblical studies. He also teaches as an adjunct professor in the School of Business Management.

In 2008 Jason cofounded Liberty Jane Clothing with his wife, Cinnamon, and serves as the company's primary marketer. To date, Liberty Jane Clothing has had over 150,000 digital guidebooks downloaded from its e-commerce website. It is a thriving six-figure online business. With a cultlike social media following, Liberty Jane has grown to include a Facebook fan page of over 14,000 likers, a YouTube channel with over 7,600 subscribers and 1.2 million video views. In 2011 the company launched its Pinterest profile, which quickly became its top source of social media traffic.

In 2011 Jason started www.marketingonpinterest.com, a blog dedicated to helping small-business owners and marketers grow their businesses on Pinterest. His Pinterest Boot Camps and free e-book *The Ultimate Pinterest Marketing Guide* have led the industry.

Jason also has an active consulting practice and loves helping entrepreneurs go from concept to cash. In 2011 he worked with over 600 small-business owners to launch or grow their new businesses. As a conference speaker and workshop leader, Jason has conducted sessions on Pinterest abroad. More information is available at http://www.pinterestpower.com.

 **Karen Lacey** is the author of *The Complete Idiot's Guide to Elance* (release date August 2012), a how-to book for the small-business owner and freelancer. Prior to this, she ran her own successful online freelance writing, ghostwriting, and editing business. During this time Karen wrote four self-help books, converted three screenplays into novels, one of which placed in a national competition, and edited and proofread countless other books and articles. She also became editor in chief for an active website promoting a variety of political views.

Karen has lived and written throughout the world. She spent seven years as a wildlife photographer and writer in southern Africa, and after moving to London she spent two years writing daily financial analyses for a boutique investment firm. She also made appearances on *Sky Business News* and *Reuters TV* and conducted daily commentaries on *Bloomberg News*. Karen has also written two novels and countless short stories and is a 2011 graduate of the Odyssey Writing Workshop. Visit Karen at http://www.pinterestpower.com or http://www.karenlaceywriter.com.